Typeset by Tek-Art Ltd, Kent
and printed in Great Britain by
The Bath Press
Bath,
for the publishers
B.T. Batsford Ltd
4 Fitzhardinge Street
London W1H 0AH

ISBN 0 7134 5730 9

Acknowledgments

The author and publisher would like to thank the
following for kind permission to reproduce illustrations
in this book: The Bridgeman Art Library for page 5; The
British Museum for page 56; The BBC Hulton Picture
Library for pages 6, 17(b), 35, 49; Collection Viollet for
page 57; The Mary Evans Picture Library for pages 22,
33(b); The Mandel Archive for pages 16(b), 37(b), 38;
The Mansell Collection for pages 5, 12, 13, 15, 16(a),
17(a), 20, 24, 26, 27, 30, 33(a), 37(a), 41, 42, 43, 46, 48,
52(a), 52(b), 55, 58(a), 58(b), 59, 60. The maps on
pages 10 and 14 were drawn by Robert Brien. All
illustrations otherwise copyright B.T. Batsford.

Frontispiece *The rising and setting sun of Napoleon.*

Cover Illustrations

(*top left*) *Le Dix Huit Brumaire* by Bouchot (courtesy
Mansell Collection); (*top right*) *Napoleon crossing the Alps*
by J.L. David (courtesy Bridgeman Art Library);
(*bottom right*) Napoleon Buonaparte by Captain Dodgin
(courtesy Mansell Collection); (*bottom left*) *The plum
pudding in danger...* (courtesy BBC Hulton Picture
Library); (*centre left*) *Napoleon Bonaparte and his family*
(courtesy Mansell Collection).

REPUTATIONS

NAPOLEON

Nathaniel Harris

B.T. BATSFORD LTD, LONDON

Contents

Time Chart

1769	Napoleon Bonaparte born at Ajaccio, Corsica.
1778	Napoleon sent to France. At Autun and Brienne military academy.
1784	Cadet at the Ecole Militaire, Paris.
1785	Commissioned lieutenant of artillery and stationed with regiment at Valence. Spends much time 1785-8 in Paris and Corsica.
1789	Beginning of French Revolution. Napoleon at Auxonne.
1790-3	Napoleon spends much time in Corsica.
1792	Second partition of Poland. France at war with Austria and Prussia. Fall of monarchy.
1793	Execution of Louis XVI. France at war with Britain. Bonapartes driven from Corsica. Napoleon at Toulon.
1794	Fall of Robespierre. Napoleon under arrest for a time.
1795	'Whiff of grapeshot' (Vendémiaire). Establishment of Directory. Prussia makes peace. Poland partitioned for third time; ceases to exist.
1796	Napoleon marries Josephine.
1796-7	Napoleon's first Italian campaign.
1798	Napoleon leads expedition to Egypt. French fleet destroyed at battle of Nile (Nelson).
1799	Napoleon returns from Egypt, seizes power in France (Brumaire). Consulate established.
1800	Napoleon defeats Austrians at Marengo. Moreau victorious at Hohenlinden.
1801	Austria makes peace at Lunéville. Napoleon agrees Concordat with Papacy. Nelson defeats Danes.
1802	Treaty of Amiens: Anglo-French peace.
1803	War between Britain and France renewed.
1804	Napoleon becomes Emperor of the French. Execution of Duc d'Enghien.
1805	Napoleon victorious against Austrians and Russians at Austerlitz. Franco-Spanish fleet defeated at Trafalgar by Nelson.
1806	Confederation of the Rhine set up; end of Holy Roman Empire. French defeat Prussians at Jena and Auerstädt. Berlin Decree: beginning of Continental System.
1807	Battles of Eylau and Friedland lead to Franco-Russian alliance at Tilsit. Napoleon sets up French-protected Grand Duchy of Warsaw. British bombard Copenhagen.
1808	Napoleon makes brother Joseph king of Spain. Fierce Spanish resistance and arrival of British expeditionary force in Portugal. Napoleon intervenes but leaves (January 1809) because of Austrian threat.
1809	War with Austrians, who are defeated at Wagram. Disastrous British expedition to Walcheren. Napoleon divorces Josephine.
1810	Napoleon marries Austrian princess Marie-Louise. Napoleon annexes Holland.
1811	Birth of Napoleon's son by Marie-Louise, the King of Rome. French driven from Portugal.
1812	Napoleon invades Russia; Grand Army destroyed.
1813	Prussia and Austria ally with Russia and Britain. Napoleon defeated at Leipzig. Wellington victorious in Spain. Allies begin invasion of France.
1814	Napoleon abdicates, becomes ruler of Elba.
1815	Napoleon returns: the 'Hundred Days', ending in defeat at Waterloo and second abdication. Napoleon taken to St Helena as British prisoner.
1821	Death of Napoleon.
1840	Napoleon's ashes taken back to France.

The Reputation

Napoleon, the Man of Destiny

'After all, what a romance my life has been!' exclaimed Napoleon Bonaparte when he looked back on his career. It was a fair appraisal. In his own time, Napoleon dazzled the world with his military victories and his making and unmaking of kingdoms. He dominated Continental Europe, and altered its frontiers according to his will, in a fashion that had not been seen for the previous thousand years. The effect was enhanced by the glamour of his personality, which combined a brooding presence – deeply appealing to the Romantic Era of the early nineteenth century – with an

Napoleon as hero and superman, triumphant. This brilliant propagandist painting, by the French artist J.L. David, shows a romanticized Napoleon leading his troops over the Alps. This feat had been accomplished by two earlier conquerors, Hannibal and Charlemagne, whose names are carved into the rocks beneath the hooves of the First Consul's rearing mount.

Napoleon as the 'Corsican Ogre', at bay. A British cartoon portraying him as a monkey, being brought down by the Russian bear and the British bulldog.

apparently inexhaustible capacity for dynamic action. All this, coloured by Napoleon's forceful language and command of the flamboyant gesture, gave his life an epic quality which was rounded off by its climax in defeat and distant exile.

During his lifetime, Napoleon was simply 'the Corsican Ogre' to some of his enemies – notably the British. But as the immediate antagonism faded, the extraordinary nature of the Napoleonic epic imposed itself on even the British mind. Within a generation or so, the Napoleonic legend seemed established everywhere, and when Queen Victoria visited Les Invalides in Paris, she instructed her son – later King Edward VII – to 'kneel down before the tomb of the great Napoleon'.

Where Napoleon is concerned, we can speak of a legend rather than a mere reputation; as we shall see, Napoleon himself played a great part in shaping it. Despite some variations over time and place, the essential shape of the legend has remained almost unchanged. It can be summarized roughly as follows:

Napoleon Bonaparte was a child of the French Revolution (1789-99), which convulsed France and challenged the old European order of privileged aristocracies and established monarchies. Although not in the fullest sense a Frenchman, the Corsican-born Bonaparte became the finest commander of the Revolutionary armies, and then made himself master of republican France. He saved the country from her foreign enemies, stabilized French society and consolidated the gains of the Revolution. In the process, Revolutionary aspirations to political liberty were sacrificed, and the Republic itself disappeared when Bonaparte made himself Emperor of France. However, the 'upstart soldier' proved to be a ruler and law-maker of genius. His victories over the European powers gave him control over the Continent, where he enthroned many of his relations and followers. Only Britain remained his irreconcilable foe. Napoleon attempted to defeat her by closing all the ports of Europe to British goods, but this led to economic difficulties which made his regime unpopular. It also helped to stimulate the feelings of national identity which were beginning to be apparent in various parts of Europe. According to Napoleon's version of his own legend, he had encouraged nationalism and intended to create a harmonious, parliamentary, nation-based United States of Europe once Britain was defeated; others have seen nationalism as purely and simply a reaction against French oppression. Either way, the legend attributes to awakening national feeling a key role in bringing down the French Emperor. Napoleon came to grief at each end of the Continent – in Spain, where a fierce guerrilla war pinned down huge numbers of troops and bled their strength; and, catastrophically, in Russia, where the dreadful winter is said to have destroyed the Napoleonic Grand Army. In the wake of this debacle, German nationalism revived and, after further defeats, Napoleon was forced to abdicate and was sent to the Mediterranean island of Elba. He made a spectacular return to France and took power again, but was decisively beaten by the Duke of Wellington at Waterloo – a defeat that the more Napoleon-worshipping devotees of the legend have tended to blame on the Emperor's failing health or incompetent subordinates. Napoleon ended his days 'chained to a rock', a British prisoner on the tiny mid-Atlantic island of St Helena.

The Napoleonic legend still exerts a potent appeal. There have been greater wars and equally powerful dictators since Napoleon's day, but the bloodshed, savagery and crimes associated with them have, if anything, made Napoleon's image more attractive. And although worship of the hero-warrior is now less whole-hearted than it was before 1914, the age of plumes, epaulettes, sabres and cannon has come to seem romantic and relatively harmless by comparison with our own nuclear age.

But what lies behind the legend and the glamour of Napoleon? Like most popular reputations, that of Napoleon Bonaparte contains one or two facts that are wrong, and many general ideas that, on investigation, seem questionable, or at least over-simple. Among the issues that might be raised are: Did Napoleon consolidate the French Revolution or destroy it? Did France *need* to be 'saved' by him? Was he an insatiable military adventurer, or were his wars forced on him by a hostile Europe? Did Britain stand out against his tyranny or simply seek to destroy France as a rival imperialist power? Was he defeated by nationalist feeling or regular armies? Did he fail because of this? or because he exhausted France and himself? or because there were fundamental weaknesses in the Napoleonic system of warfare?

Such questions are what this book is about. Having looked hard at Napoleon's reputation, readers will probably think that it needs some modification. But they are still likely to feel that the Napoleonic adventure constituted one of the most remarkable episodes in European history.

The Background

An Age of Revolution and War

A spectacular career such as Napoleon's is only possible in an age of upheaval. In ordinary times, even the most gifted man or woman rises slowly in the world and must set limits to his or her ambitions.

The state of Europe

Until the outbreak of the French Revolution in 1789 – when Napoleon was 20 years old – the stable, tradition-minded European order provided no opportunities for a military adventurer to seize a throne and turn the world upside down. All the great powers were monarchies, ruled by long-established dynasties such as the Bourbons in France. Almost everywhere, the land-owning aristocracy dominated society, which was largely governed by custom and tradition. As well as titles and wealth, nobles enjoyed many legal and economic privileges; and, among other things, they monopolized the important positions in the army, the Church and politics. The monarch sometimes tried to limit aristocratic privileges in order to increase the power of the state, and then a conflict might ensue. But such quarrels were usually settled by compromise, and there was little thought of changing the social order. This was the old order – the Ancien Régime – overthrown by the French Revolution.

The international order was also slow to change. Eighteenth-century wars were fought for limited objectives – to gain a province rather than to overthrow a rival monarch or destroy his state. Powers waxed and waned, and the outlines on the map of Europe did alter, but over centuries rather than years.

The Bourbons had inherited the French crown in 1589.

The French Revolution

All this was changed by the French Revolution. In 1789, King Louis XVI of France was bankrupt. Having failed to persuade his nobles to pay reasonable taxes, he was desperate enough to summon the Estates General – an elected assembly whose existence had almost been forgotten. But Louis got far more than he had bargained for. Given a voice, the educated middle class demanded political reforms and an end to aristocratic privilege. Combined with pressure from an aroused peasantry and discontented town workers, this led to a revolution in which privilege was abolished and the King became a constitutional sovereign. But, once begun, revolutions are not easy to stop. The divisions between Frenchmen widened rather than narrowed. Neither Louis nor his nobles were really prepared to accept the new state of affairs, while the various revolutionary factions increasingly disagreed about how far the revolution should go. In the struggles that ensued, there was a mass emigration of the nobles; and these *émigrés* soon formed a hostile menacing force beyond France's frontiers. Then, in January 1793, the revolutionaries burned their boats by executing the King and transforming France into a republic.

A constitution is essentially a set of rules controlling the way in which a country's political affairs are conducted. Unlike an 'absolute' monarch or dictator, a constitutional sovereign (whether King or Assembly) must operate within such rules.

France at war

France was already at war with three major powers – Britain, Austria and Prussia – but the execution of a fellow-monarch was seen as a direct challenge to everything the crowned heads of Europe stood for. The war now took on a bitter ideological aspect; the old order was determined to stamp on 'the hydra of revolution', while the French threatened to revolutionize their enemies' territories, promising 'fraternal aid' to any people that rose to claim its liberty.

France seemed to be in a hopeless position as most of Europe massed forces against her, since Britain, Austria and Prussia were soon joined in this 'First Coalition' by Holland, Spain and the Italian state of Piedmont. Furthermore, the French army was in disarray because most of the nobly-born officer class hated the Revolution and had joined the *émigrés*. This situation enabled a gifted but obscure officer like Napoleon Bonaparte to fill one vacancy after another, and to become a general at the age of 24; but for the most part it deprived the army of experienced men and seriously weakened discipline.

However, France was a country with exceptional resources. She was fertile and wealthy, and her population was the largest of any European state except Russia; by the late eighteenth century, there were roughly 28 million Frenchmen by comparison with about nine million Englishmen and a mere three million Prussians. These advantages had been the basis of French attempts to dominate Europe within the framework of the old order, and of the general recognition of France as 'the Great Nation' during the reign of Louis XIV (1643-1715). They persisted under the Revolution; and now, faced with the First Coalition, France's armies were charged with a new kind of energy, partly inspired by national enthusiasm and partly stimulated by the centralized control of resources brought about by the Revolution. In 1793, by introducing mass conscription for the first time in modern history, the French Republic matched the European armies in numbers and succeeded in driving them back. Soon French conquests would begin to alter the map of Europe.

Political geography

During the early years of the French Revolution, there were five great European powers on that map: France, Austria, Prussia, Russia and Britain. Austria was a multi-national empire, reigned over by the ancient Habsburg dynasty and based on a large bloc of territory in the heart of Europe which corresponded roughly to modern Austria, Hungary and Czechoslovakia. The Habsburgs ruled or indirectly controlled much of Italy, which was divided into a number of separate states, and Belgium was also a Habsburg province (the Austrian Netherlands). Germany too was fragmented, though her 300-odd independent units were nominally part of the Holy Roman Empire, a loose political association almost a thousand years old. The Holy Roman Emperor was always the head of the Austrian Habsburg dynasty, but the title carried so little authority that from 1804 the Habsburgs also used a more realistic title, Emperors of Austria.

The other great German power was Prussia, whose kings had devoted all the resources of their relatively poor state to the creation of an army of legendary prowess. Russia was a backward but vast country whose emperors, or Tsars, ruled autocratically; their interventions in European affairs were erratic though sometimes forceful and effective.

Unlike the other European powers, Britain relied on her splendid navy in wartime, and mounted only small-scale military expeditions to the Continent. Thanks to her thriving commerce, she could afford to finance

Hydra of revolution: in mythology, the hydra was a many-headed monster – an apt image of revolution from a conservative point of view.

Conscription: compulsory military service.

HABSBURG LANDS

RUSSIAN EMPIRE

PAPAL STATES

VENETIAN REPUBLIC

KINGDOM OF SARDINIA

BOUNDARY OF
HOLY ROMAN EMPIRE

*Europe in 1789 before the French
Revolution.*

her Continental allies, whose armies bore the brunt of any fighting against
the common enemy. Most of the time – even long before the Revolution –
this meant France, the only state capable of competing economically with
Britain or dominating Europe and launching a cross-Channel invasion. In
Britain, as in other countries, the aristocracy were in the ascendant, but
Britain was a constitutional state and a relatively open society.
Nonetheless, British radicals, inspired by the French Revolution, hoped to
win greater liberty – just one more reason why British governments
remained as hostile to Revolutionary and Napoleonic France as they had
been to her Bourbon predecessors. Throughout Napoleon's career, Britain
was to be his implacable enemy, financing one coalition after another
against him until his downfall.

The rise of Napoleon

The First Coalition against Revolutionary France (1793-7) collapsed when faced with the ferocious response of the conscript armies – 'the nation in arms'. After their early victories, the French annexed Belgium (1794) and transformed Holland into the Batavian Republic (1795), the first 'fraternal' state with a constitution modelled on that of France. In 1795 Prussia withdrew from the war; then in 1796-7 French victories drove the Austrians from Italy. Northern Italy was organized into French-style republics, the Austrians were forced to make peace, and Britain was left without allies on the Continent.

Inside France, political crises continued to occur. The energetic and efficient organization of the country for war in 1793 was the work of a revolutionary dictatorship, exercised by radical republicans known as Jacobins. But the internal 'Terror' organized by Maximilien Robespierre and other Jacobins got out of hand, and their increasingly free use of the guillotine against suspected counter-revolutionaries and political rivals produced a reaction after the fall of Robespierre in July 1794. In the following year a more moderate revolutionary regime, the Directory (1795-9), was set up.

Paul Barras, one of the five Directors who ran the new government, discovered a young general of genius in Napoleon Bonaparte. Bonaparte had first made his mark in 1793 at the siege of Toulon, France's great southern port, which had been occupied by the British. The young artillery officer had been chiefly responsible for dislodging them, and had been promoted to brigadier-general at the age of 24. Then he had helped Barras to crush a royalist uprising in Paris (1795), positioning artillery so that 'a whiff of grapeshot' decimated and dispersed the rebels. He was rewarded with the command of the Army of Italy, and it was Napoleon Bonaparte whose dazzlingly successful campaign in 1796-7 drove out the Austrians.

Bonaparte was young, ambitious, popular and uncomfortably high-handed in his behaviour – all good reasons why the Directors were glad to get rid of him by sending him to Egypt. The object of the expedition was to gain a new colony for France and to disrupt British communications with the East. But despite a number of victories, Bonaparte achieved little. The French were almost immediately cut off from Europe by the battle of Aboukir Bay (1 August 1798), where their ships were destroyed by a British fleet commanded by Horatio Nelson. Advancing against the Turks, Bonaparte's army failed to capture Acre and was driven back into Egypt by an outbreak of plague. Eventually Bonaparte left the army behind and slipped back to France, where the political situation was critical. On 9 November 1799 – 18 Brumaire in France's Revolutionary calendar – he overthrew the Directory and installed a new regime, the Consulate.

Guillotine: Device used in France for beheading criminals.

The Revolutionary calendar. The French Revolutionists believed they were ushering in a new age of reason and breaking with the 'superstitious' past. One of their measures was to introduce a new 'metric' calendar on 22 September 1792, which became the first day of the Year 1. Weeks consisted of 10 days, and the new months were given climatically appropriate names: Brumaire (22 October to 20 November) signified 'month of fog' and Thermidor (19 July to 17 August) 'month of heat'.

The battle of Lodi (1796), one of the dazzling victories won by Napoleon during his first Italian campaign.

From simple soldier to Emperor. The presence of the Pope and the splendour of the ceremonial were employed to make Napoleon's new role as awe-inspiring – and seemingly God-given – as possible. This painting by J.L. David has the same intention: it shows him in full majesty, crowning his wife Josephine.

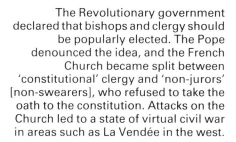

The Revolutionary government declared that bishops and clergy should be popularly elected. The Pope denounced the idea, and the French Church became split between 'constitutional' clergy and 'non-jurors' [non-swearers], who refused to take the oath to the constitution. Attacks on the Church led to a state of virtual civil war in areas such as La Vendée in the west.

Consul and Emperor

Instead of five Directors, there were now three Consuls. Bonaparte was First Consul – and soon, thanks to a string of successes, he was the only one that mattered. He recovered the French position in Italy by a narrowly won but decisive victory over the Austrians at Marengo (June 1800); and when the Austrians were defeated again, this time in central Europe by General Moreau at Hohenlinden (December 1800), they were forced to make peace with France at Lunéville (February 1801). Meanwhile, Bonaparte had begun a substantial reorganization of French society, codifying the laws, stabilizing the economy, ending France's quarrel with the Roman Catholic Church, quelling the last royalist resistance inside the country and encouraging *émigrés* to return. For a time, his policy of peace and reconciliation seemed complete, since an Anglo-French treaty was signed at Amiens in 1802. But disputes between the two countries continued, and in 1803 the war was resumed.

For more than a year, Bonaparte's ambitious plans for a cross-Channel invasion hung fire because of Britain's command of the sea. Meanwhile, in 1804 he made himself Emperor of France as Napoleon I. He revived the title 'Marshal of France' and conferred it on his finest generals – men such as Murat, Ney, Davout, Augereau, Bernadotte, Macdonald, Masséna and Soult, who were to play prominent roles in the Napoleonic epic. In time an imperial nobility was created, and few vestiges of the republic were allowed to remain. Republics also disappeared elsewhere in Europe: Napoleon became King of Italy, and France's other satellites were persuaded to offer thrones to his relatives and most able followers. But although the Church and the monarchy had reappeared in France, there was no return to the Ancien Régime's fixed system of privileges. By comparison with the situation in other parts of Continental Europe, the 'career open to talents' in France, and Napoleonic institutions in general, still seemed progressive enough to provide a justification for French expansion.

Years of victory

Over the next few years, Napoleon became the dominant figure in Europe. Nelson's victory at Trafalgar (October 1805) made Britain secure from invasion, but on land Napoleon's Grand Army rapidly defeated her allies. Austria made peace after the battle of Austerlitz (December 1805), generally regarded as Napoleon's most brilliant victory, and Prussia's supposedly crack armies were crushed at Jena and Auerstädt (1806).

The Imperial Guard enters Paris through a triumphal arch after the victorious campaign against Prussia – a familiar scene during Napoleon's years of glory.

Napoleon completely reorganized Germany, turning most of western Germany into the French-patronized Confederation of the Rhine; the ancient Holy Roman Empire disappeared from history. The Russians remained in the field and inflicted heavy casualties on the Grand Army at Eylau (February 1807), but were defeated four months later at Friedland; after a famous meeting between Napoleon and the Tsar Alexander, a Franco-Russian alliance was signed at Tilsit in July 1807.

Now at the height of his power, Napoleon decided that the only way to defeat Britain was by economic warfare. He set up the 'Continental System', a blockade that was intended to ruin Britain's industry and commerce by keeping British goods out of Europe. The British retaliated, and over the next few years the struggle took its toll of both powers; Britain was hard hit, but the lack of British goods caused economic problems on the Continent that made Napoleon's political system much less popular.

Napoleon's other policies also produced an unexpected amount of unrest. In 1808 he bullied the Spanish king into giving up his crown, which passed to Napoleon's older brother, Joseph Bonaparte. But the Spanish people were fiercely attached to their traditional way of life and rose in a spontaneous revolt against the French presence in their country. Though defeated in battle, they conducted a long-drawn-out guerrilla war that pinned down huge numbers of French troops and made it possible for a British expeditionary force to establish itself in neighbouring Portugal. Napoleon was later to claim that 'It was the Spanish ulcer that ruined me.'

The French were also unpopular in parts of north Germany, where nationalist feeling was just beginning to develop. When Austria again went to war with France, there were anti-French outbreaks in Germany and a full-scale peasant rising in the Tyrol, which had been taken from Austria and given to France's ally, Bavaria. But Napoleon's victory at the battle of Wagram forced the Austrians to make peace and doomed the risings. Despite the 'Spanish ulcer', Napoleon remained the master of Europe and was able to consolidate his position in 1810 by divorcing his wife, Josephine, and marrying Marie-Louise, the daughter of the Austrian Emperor. When she bore him a son, who was given the title 'King of Rome', it seemed that Napoleon had succeeded in founding a secure imperial line.

By 1812, however, Napoleon's alliance with the Tsar had broken down, and he decided to invade Russia – with disastrous consequences. His huge Grand Army thrust deep into the country and, after a bloody but indecisive engagement at Borodino, pressed on as far as Moscow. But since the Tsar refused to negotiate, the French found themselves stranded in the smouldering ruins of the city and, with provisions dwindling and winter coming on, had no alternative but to retreat. Hungry, frostbitten and constantly harassed by the Russians, the Grand Army disintegrated.

After this disaster, Napoleon's fortunes declined steadily. He was still capable of winning brilliant victories, but the balance of forces in Europe had shifted decisively against him. Prussia, eager for revenge, joined the Russians, and when it became apparent that they were likely to win, Austria changed sides. The recall of French troops from Spain allowed the British to take the offensive there; they were commanded by Sir Arthur Wellesley, later created Duke of Wellington. The German Confederation collapsed, Napoleon's remaining allies deserted him, and by 1814 France herself was being invaded. After the fall of Paris, Napoleon's marshals refused to carry on the struggle, and in April 1814 he was forced to abdicate.

Europe in 1810, when Napoleon was at the height of his power.

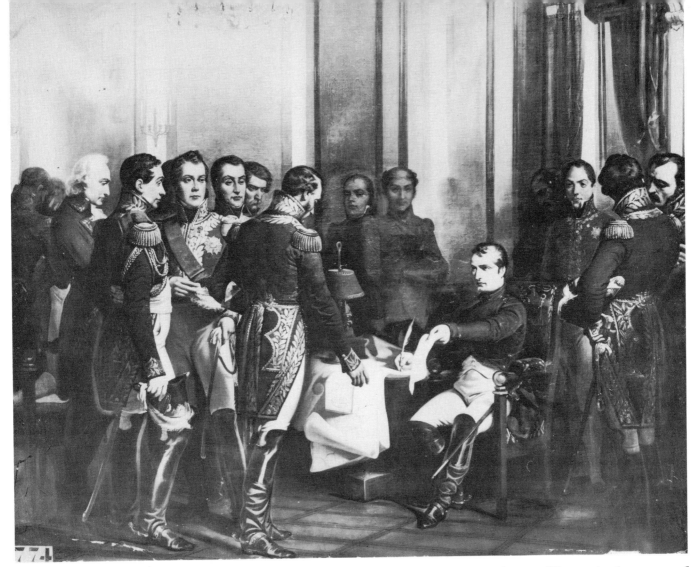

Defeat: Napoleon abdicates for the first time in 1814. Like so many nineteenth-century paintings, this one is meticulous in its rendering of detail but unconvincingly melodramatic and incurably romantic – in this instance through its glamorous portrayal of Napoleon, who by 1814 was in fact corpulent and balding.

The Bourbon dynasty was restored to the throne of France in the person of Louis XVIII, while Napoleon was allowed to remain a sovereign, being given the little Mediterranean island of Elba as his domain.

But Napoleon's amazing career was not yet over. The Bourbons quickly made themselves unpopular, and the victorious allies quarrelled so violently that a new war seemed possible. Seizing his opportunity, in February 1815 Napoleon returned to France, where he was rapturously received and again swept to power. However, it soon became clear that the allies would close ranks against him. Hoping to defeat the British under Wellington and the Prussians under Blücher before further allied armies arrived, Napoleon marched into Belgium. But his defeat at Waterloo (June 1815) effectively ended his reign, and after a second abdication he was exiled to the island of St Helena in the middle of the Atlantic.

Between 1815 and his death in 1821, Napoleon busied himself in trying to create his own legend through recorded conversations and dictated memoirs. His version of events, which portrayed him as an essentially benevolent and liberal figure, is only one aspect of the reputation which we are now about to examine.

Interpretations

The Young Bonaparte

Realist or Romantic?

Napoleon had a more complicated and interesting personality than most men of action. To satisfy his craving for power, he had to be a supreme realist; but there were several other sides to his nature, including a vein of romanticism that inclined him to grandiose and exotic dreams. Odd contradictions crop up in any examination of his career: for example, he was a Corsican patriot who made himself master of France; a revolutionary who loathed mobs and became a despot; and a self-absorbed egoist who loved his family and knew how to win, lead and inspire followers.

The circumstances of Napoleon's childhood and youth help to account for some aspects of his personality. He was born on 15 August 1769 at Ajaccio, a little town on the relatively poor and primitive island of Corsica. The Corsicans were Italians in language and culture, and down to 1768 the island had belonged to the Italian republic of Genoa. But in that year

Napoleon's father, Carlo Buonaparte (or, in French, Charles Bonaparte) and his mother, Letizia, a formidable character whose refrain during his years of power was 'If it lasts!'

Genoa sold Corsica to France, which quickly crushed Corsican resistance; and so Napoleon was born a Frenchman, though known for some time by the Italian form of his name, Napoleone Buonaparte.

Napoleon's parents, Carlo and Letizia Buonaparte, were Corsican nobles who had taken part in the resistance to France. After its collapse, Carlo made his peace with the new regime – which was just as well, since he was perpetually hard up and had an increasingly large family to support (Napoleon eventually had seven surviving brothers and sisters). One of the privileges of noble status under the Ancien Régime was a claim on the royal bounty, and when Napoleon was nine years old he learned French for a few months at Autun and then entered the military college at Brienne as a King's scholar.

French myth-making: Napoleon's uncle is said to be predicting that he, not his older brother Joseph, will become the head of the family. The artist has even made the small boy tuck his hand into his tunic in 'Napoleonic' fashion!

English myth-making: here Napoleon and his family are starvelings, and the future Emperor is shown as owing his advancement to the King's bounty.

DEMOCRATIC INNOCENCE

The young Buonaparte & his wretched Relatives, in their native Poverty, while Free Booters in the Island of Corsica.

DEMOCRATIC HUMILITY.

Buonaparte when a boy received thro' the King's bounty into the Ecole Militaire at Paris.

LIFE OF BUONAPARTE.

The next few years were hard ones. As a poor 'foreigner' with a peculiar accent, Napoleon was laughed at by his wealthy aristocratic schoolmates, and seeing his parents only once in every few years intensified his feeling of isolation. Driven in on himself, he became a passionate reader and a dreamer; and he clung to his foreignness, longing for Corsican independence even while entering the Royal Military College in Paris, graduating, and taking up garrison duty as a 16-year-old officer at Valence. Even after the outbreak of the French Revolution in 1789, he wrote a blood-thirsty tale of massacre and revenge, 'New Corsica', in which the main character declares:

> I was born in Corsica, and grew up with a violent love for my unfortunate country and for her independence. At that time we were languishing in the fetters of the Genoese . . . . After various changes of fortune, Paoli di Rostino became first magistrate and generalissimo. We expelled our tyrants. We were free, we were happy; then the French, who are often called enemies of free men, came armed with fire and sword. In two years they had compelled Paoli to leave and the nation to surrender.
> Translated by Christopher Frayling in his book *Napoleon Wrote Fiction*, Compton Press, 1972.

Paoli di Rostino is usually called Pasquale di Paoli in English-speaking countries. He lived in exile in England from 1769 to 1789.

Napoleon also wrote to Paoli that 'I was born as our country was dying. Thirty thousand Frenchmen spewed on to our coasts, drowning the throne of liberty in rivers of blood.'

The high-flown style in which Napoleon wrote was typically romantic. The impact of the Romantic movement was felt throughout Europe, and it involved more than a change of style: Romanticism was a new state of mind, involving a revolt against the everyday and hard common sense. Along with a rapturous response to untamed nature, the primitive and the exotic, went a taste for inwardness and a cult of passion – the exploration of the untamed and unsocial sides of the human personality. At 16, Napoleon wrote of himself in Romantic vein, 'Always alone in the midst of men, I return home to dream, and to surrender to my melacholy in all its variety.' And a few years later, in a fragment of a novel, *Clisson and Eugénie*, he makes his warrior hero retire from active life:

The Romantic movement is best known in Britain through poets such as Wordsworth and Coleridge. In France, Jean-Jacques Rousseau's cult of nature and admiration for primitive 'unspoiled' peoples such as the Corsicans was immensely influential – on, among other things, Napoleons's rhapsodic style.

> He knew no more agreeable pastime than to wander in the woods. There he found contentment, he could defy small-mindedness and rise above the folly and the baseness of humanity.
> Sometimes, on silver starlit banks, he surrendered to the desires of his trembling heart. He could no longer tear himself from the sweet but melancholy spectacle of a moonlit night. He would often remain there until the moon had vanished from sight and darkness had effaced his reverie; sad and uneasy, he would then depart in search of a much needed repose.
> Quoted in Frayling, *Napoleon Wrote Fiction*.

However, the romantic dreamer was drawn into a life of action by the outbreak of the French Revolution. For several years Corsica – not Paris – continued to absorb most of his thoughts. In the new atmosphere of freedom, Paoli was able to return in triumph to the island, and Napoleon managed to spend most of his time there in spite of his military duties. But the conservative Paoli disliked revolutionary ideas and hoped to make Corsica independent under British protection. The Bonapartes opposed him, with Napoleon taking the lead. After a series of complicated intrigues and faction-fights, the Paolists were victorious. In June 1793 the Bonapartes were driven into exile, and from this time onwards Napoleon sought to make a career as a citizen and soldier of France. Corsica disappeared so completely from his mind (if we can judge from what he said

Since the death of his father in 1785 Napoleon had become the effective head of the family; his older brother, Joseph, was a much less forceful character.

and wrote) that some historians have dismissed his Corsican patriotism as no more than the play-acting of a careerist. On the other hand, there was not much he could do to or for his native island, since it remained under British occupation from 1794 to 1796.

Corsica was only one of several parts of France that had revolted against the Republic in 1793. In the west, La Vendée had risen for the royalist cause, whereas Marseille and other southern cities stood out against the radical Jacobin government in the name of a more conservative republicanism. Soon after his return from Corsica, Napoleon wrote a pamphlet, *Supper in Beaucaire*, against the Marseillais:

Marseillais: The inhabitants of Marseille.

> What effect has your movement produced on the Republic? You have led it almost to ruin, you have hampered our army operations. I do not know if you have been in the pay of the Spaniard and the Austrian, but they certainly could not have wished for a happier diversion. What more could you do if you were in their pay? Every well-known aristocrat is anxious for your success. You have put avowed aristocrats at the head of your administration and your armies. . . . Your battalions are full of such people and your cause would not be theirs if it was that of the Republic.
> Quoted in Frayling, *Napoleon Wrote Fiction*.

Napoleon asserted that it was wrong for the Marseillais to resist a government they disliked, because their actions would help the enemies of the Republic. Do you think this is a valid argument?

Napoleon's tone here is sober and hard-headed. He writes shorter, crisper sentences, aiming to drive his point home rather than express emotions: this is Napoleon the realist. *Supper in Beaucaire* is presented in the form of a dialogue, a debate in which several points of view are expressed – although, since it is essentially a work of propaganda, it is always clear that the Marseillais are losing the argument. When speaking for himself, Napoleon (who figures in the dialogue as The Soldier) avoids emotional appeals to republican principles and liberty, which in this period could be every bit as high-flown as the romantic writings quoted earlier. He confronts the Marseillais with the realities – that they are bound to lose, and that by holding out they are risking the prosperity of their famous and ancient city:

> Let poorer regions fight to the last ditch; the inhabitant of the Vivarais, of the Cevennes, and of Corsica will expose himself fearlessly to the outcome of battle; if he wins, he has achieved his goal, if he loses he finds himself in the position to make peace in exactly the same circumstances as before.
> . . . But you!. . . you lose one battle and the fruit of a thousand years of hard work, exertion, thrift and happiness become the soldier's prey.
> Quoted in Frayling, *Napoleon Wrote Fiction*.

Can you find other examples of Napoleon's 'romantic' and 'realist' sides in the extracts given in other chapters?

In time, Napoleon's style became more staccato – the instrument of an all-powerful commander rapping out orders and judgments. As action and the exercise of power became the mainsprings of his life, the realist – or bully – took control, and with the years his judgment of men and affairs tended to become more and more contemptuously cynical. Yet the Romantic in Napoleon still appeared from time to time, in his mystical belief in his 'star' or destiny, and in the romantic taste for the exotic East, which, it can be argued, inspired his Egyptian expedition. Above all, Napoleon was romantic about war and 'glory' – the fame and glamour attached to being a great warrior; and it was this that enabled him to appeal to his soldiers in thrillingly expressed proclamations, and on occasion to behave in a high heroic style quite unexpected in a man who boasted that all his actions were dictated by calculation.

Republican hero?

Napoleon's expulsion from Corsica turned out to be a great stroke of luck. Revolutionary France was a politically unstable society, full of dangers; but it also offered exceptional opportunities – especially to a soldier who was prepared to serve the Republic. Large numbers of the old aristocratic officer class had left France since the Revolution, and there was a shortage of trained military men; so a talented professional such as Napoleon Bonaparte was likely to go far, unless he became identified with the wrong political viewpoint.

Thanks to this situation, Napoleon's protracted absences in Corsica had been tolerated by the military authorities, and he had even been promoted. But he made his first real mark in 1793, shortly after his return to France, when he was employed at the siege of Toulon, the great southern seaport which was occupied by the British. Napoleon distinguished himself by his skilful use of artillery, and it was his plan that led to the capture of a key fort; immediately after this, realizing that the city was now indefensible, the British evacuated it.

As a reward, Napoleon was made a brigadier-general. He had made his political loyalties clear in *Supper in Beaucaire*, which was printed by order of the government, and he soon became friendly with Augustin Robespierre, whose brother Maximilien was one of the leading Jacobins. Since the Robespierres showed considerable interest in Napoleon's plans for an invasion of Italy, the young brigadier seemed certain of rapid advancement.

The young Napoleon, lean and long-haired, after the Revolutionary fashion. A convincing portrayal despite the element of hero-worship.

Soldats! voici la batterie des Hommes sans peur.

Though Napoleon had thrown in his lot with the Jacobins, it is hard to be sure what his real political beliefs were. As early as 1791, he wrote in a style more radical than most Jacobins that

When man is born, he brings with him the right to that portion of the fruits of the earth necessary to his existence . . . . [Later] He casts a glance around him. He sees the land shared between a few owners, serving to feed luxury and superfluity; he asks himself 'What are the claims of these men? Why does the idle man own everything, the working man practically nothing?'
From 'Discourse to the Academy of Lyon', a long essay submitted in a prize competition; translated by Frayling in *Napoleon Wrote Fiction*.

Yet less than a year later, in a letter to his older brother, Joseph, he declared that 'The Jacobins are lunatics, and have no common sense.' And to another brother, Lucien, he wrote in a confused and disillusioned fashion:

The men at the head of affairs are a poor lot. One must admit, upon closer acquaintance, that the people are hardly worth all the trouble that is taken to merit their support. You know the history of Ajaccio. That of Paris is exactly the same, though perhaps people here are pettier, viler, more abusive, and more censorious. You have to look closely before you realize that enthusiasm is still enthusiasm, and that the French are an ancient and independent people . . . . Every individual is out for his own interests, and will forward them, if he can, by insult and outrage: intrigue is as underhand as ever. All this discourages ambition.
Quoted in J.M. Thompson, *Napoleon's Letters*, Dent (Everyman's Library), 1954.

Contradictory statements such as these, together with his later behaviour as a dictator, have led some writers to assert that Napoleon was never more than a careerist with no fixed convictions. But it can also be argued that changes of mood and opinions are not unusual in a very young man – and especially during a revolutionary period when society in general is highly volatile. In Napoleon's case, there was only one political emotion that seems never to have left him: a hatred and fear of mobs, first expressed in his disgusted reactions to the events leading to the overthrow of the monarchy.

Napoleon's Jacobin links suddenly became a disadvantage in July 1794, when both Robespierres were arrested and guillotined during the *coup d'état* of Thermidor (named after the month in the revolutionary calendar). Napoleon was briefly imprisoned, and although he managed to convince his captors that he had taken no part in politics, he remained under a cloud for some time. After a period of bitter poverty in Paris, he again benefited from the shortage of skilled officers and found a powerful patron. The Army of the Interior was commanded by Paul Barras, who was a politician rather than a soldier; so when a royalist rising took place in Paris on 13 Vendémiaire (5 October 1795), Barras brought in the nearest available professional – the unemployed Bonaparte. Hastily collecting artillery and placing it strategically to protect the Convention (the French legislative assembly), Napoleon scattered the insurgents with a 'whiff of grapeshot'. He described the event in a letter to his brother Joseph:

The Convention appointed Barras to command the armed forces of the Government: the committee chose me as second in command. We disposed our troops. The enemy attacked us at the Tuileries. We killed a large number of them. They killed thirty of our men, and wounded sixty. We have disarmed the sections, and all is quiet. As usual, I haven't had a scratch.
Quoted in Thompson, *Napoleon's Letters*.

Ajaccio was the town in Corsica where Napoleon was born. See p. 16.

To evaluate historical characters and events you must decide what you believe to be 'normal'. How consistent are *your* opinions and those of people you know? How often do you change your mind about political and other matters?

Coup d'etat: a sudden, usually violent seizing of power.

Dated 2 a.m., 6 October 1795, immediately after the end of the uprising; this probably accounts for the brief, unemotional description. The Tuileries, an ex-royal palace, was where the French legislature met. The sections were Parisian local government wards, at whose meetings most popular uprisings (including this one) originated.

*Josephine Beauharnais, who married
Napoleon in 1796.*

Stendhal served on and off for some
years in the imperial administration. He
accompanied Napoleon's army in 1800
when it crossed the Alps into Italy, and
was in Moscow when the Russians
burned it in 1812.

Shortly afterwards, a new form of republican government, the Directory, was set up. Barras became one of the five Directors who governed France, and Napoleon succeeded him as Commander of the Army of the Interior. He also met and fell in love with Josephine Beauharnais, a glamorous society woman who had been Barras' mistress. Since Josephine was also a 33-year-old widow with two children, extravagant habits and little money, she encouraged the rising young general's attentions, and married him on 9 March 1796.

After a brief honeymoon, Napoleon left to take up his new command as General of the Army of Italy. The campaigns of 1796-7 are often regarded as the most brilliant of his career. Facing much larger Austrian armies, the French were often in peril, but Napoleon's swiftness of movement and tactical genius carried the day again and again. Lodi, Rivoli and Arcola were only the most famous of an unbroken series of victories that dazzled Napoleon's contemporaries. The feelings of Frenchmen were recalled long afterwards by the great writer Stendhal, who opened his novel *The Charterhouse of Parma* (1839) with the words:

On the 15th of May, 1796, General Bonaparte made his entry into Milan at the head of that young army which had shortly before crossed the bridge at Lodi and taught the world that after all these centuries Caesar and Alexander had a successor. The miracles of gallantry and genius of which Italy was a witness in the space of a few months aroused a slumbering people . . .
Translated by C.K. Scott Moncrieff.

In 1797, Napoleon's army marched out of northern Italy and deep into Habsburg territory; but the French offensives in central Europe had failed, and Napoleon boldly took it upon himself to make peace with Austria. The Directors had no choice but to agree, and the preliminary arrangements made at Leoben (18 April 1797) were confirmed at Campo Formio (18 October 1797). In return for France's gains (Belgium, the left bank of the Rhine, a pro-French regime in northern Italy), Austria was given the

Venetian Republic, which Napoleon had occupied. Although Venetian republicanism was aristocratic (that is, not of a kind sympathetic to France), Napoleon's use of this hitherto independent state as a mere bargaining counter was hardly compatible with the contemporary French picture of him as the liberator of Italy. He justified himself in harsh, practical terms:

There is no treaty between the French Republic and the municipality of Venice which obliges us to sacrifice our interests . . . . The French Republic has never made it a principle to fight for other nations . . . . No doubt it comes easily enough to a few gas-bags, who only deserve the name of fools, to call for a universal republic. I should like to see these gentry on a winter campaign. In any case, there is no such thing as a Venetian nation. Effeminate, corrupt, split up into as many divisions as there are towns, and as false as they are cowardly, the Italians are quite unfit for freedom.
Quoted in Thompson, *Napoleon's Letters*

Do Napoleon's Italian origins thrown any light on this statement?

After Campo Formio, the Continent was at peace for the time being, but France and Britain remained locked in combat. On his return from Italy, Napoleon was put in charge of the Army of England, which was intended to mount an invasion across the Channel; but he quickly realized that British naval superiority made such an enterprise terribly risky. Instead, he backed a plan for an expedition to Egypt, put forward by the French foreign minister, Talleyrand. By conquering Egypt, France would gain a valuable colony that would partly compensate her for the loss of many overseas territories to Britain; and from Egypt the French might be able to strike at Britain's communications with her Indian possessions, which were regarded as the major source of her wealth. This was, to say the least, over-optimistic, since climate, geography and British sea-power made any effective French exploitation of Egypt highly improbable. Nor was it wise to send a French army out of Europe when the Continental monarchs might return to the attack at any time. Why did the Directors agree? One member of the expedition, rapidly disillusioned by the realities of Egypt, put forward a reason which has been generally accepted:

Bonaparte, by virtue of his genius and victories won with an army which had become invincible, had too great an influence in France. He was an embarrassment, not to say an obstacle, to those who hold the reins of power. I was able to discover no other causes.
Extract from a letter written to his wife by François Bernoyer, chief of supplies to the Army of the Orient; quoted in Jean Tulard, *Napoleon: the myth of the saviour*, Weidenfeld, 1984.

However, Napoleon went willingly enough. This has usually been explained as a shrewd political decision: he is supposed to have realized that the time was not ripe to seize power, and to have taken himself out of the way until the Directory – already unpopular – had become completely discredited. However, the Egyptian expedition was an extremely risky venture, as events showed; and it was hardly prudent for a politically ambitious man to let himself be sent so far away from Paris. If some other general had seized power while Napoleon was in Egypt we should judge the expedition quite differently, and suggest a different motive for it. Napoleon, like other romantic-minded people of the time, certainly felt the lure of the (supposedly) 'mysterious East'; later he would excite the Tsar of Russia with talk of partitioning the Ottoman Turkish empire between them and marching on India. Perhaps, on this occasion, he really was inspired to act by these fantasies. Years later, he recalled

In Egypt I found myself freed from the obstacles of an irksome civilization. I was

Napoleon visiting plague-stricken French soldiers at Jaffa in Palestine. An inspired propagandist, Napoleon employed artists as well as writers to create favourable images of himself and his policies. In this engraving (after a painting by Gros) the general fearlessly touches the victims, whereas the members of his entourage muffle their faces and keep their distance.

The Koran is the holy book of Islam, the religion of Muslims. Do you think Napoleon's nostalgic account of this period is to be trusted?

full of dreams. I saw myself founding a religion, marching into Asia, riding an elephant with a turban on my head and, in my hand, a new Koran that I would have composed to suit my need. The time I spent in Egypt was the most beautiful of my life because it was the most ideal.
Quoted in David Chandler, *Napoleon*, Weidenfeld, 1973.

The expedition set out in May 1798, captured Malta en route, and by the end of July had defeated and supplanted the Mameluke rulers of Egypt. But on 1 August the French flotilla was destroyed at anchor in Aboukir Bay by a British fleet led by Horatio Nelson. The French had badly underestimated British naval strength in the Mediterranean, and the result of the (miscalled) 'battle of the Nile' was to cut Napoleon's army off from France. Then, encouraged by the news, the Turks, nominal overlords of Egypt, declared war on France. Characteristically, Napoleon seized the initiative by advancing into Palestine, capturing Jaffa and besieging Acre. But Acre held out under the able direction of a British officer, Sir Sidney Smith, and when plague broke out among his troops Napoleon retreated into Egypt. Soon after his return, he restored morale by routing the Turkish army which had landed from Rhodes. The French continued to hold Egypt, but when he became aware of what was happening in Europe, Napoleon decided he must go back to France, even though this meant leaving his army behind.

Some historians have called this a shocking act of desertion. If you want to make up your mind about it, try to discover what Napoleon's exact instructions were, what the Directory expected of him, and how he viewed the European situation.

The First Consul

The coup d'état

Napoleon left Egypt with a few trusted officers, and managed to reach France in safety in October 1799; if his ship had been captured by the patrolling British navy the history of Europe might have been very different. The news which had brought him back was that another war had broken out and was going badly for France: the British had organized a second European coalition whose offensives had brought it within striking distance of the French frontiers.

This danger had receded by the time Napoleon landed, thanks to victories in Holland and Switzerland by Brune and Masséna; but, nevertheless, all the territory conquered during Napoleon's first Italian campaign had been lost. At home, the Directory had failed to solve the economic problems that plagued France and, opposed by both royalists and Jacobins, survived only by means of limitations on the right to vote and occasional purges and 'whiffs of grapeshot'. There was a general recognition that the Directory could not last much longer, and the Directors themselves were manoeuvring in preparation for a change of regime. One in particular, the veteran revolutionary Sieyès, was looking for 'a sword' – a soldier who would carry out a *coup d'état* on his behalf. His first choice, Joubert, had been killed in battle; his second, Moreau, had declined to meddle in politics, but told Sieyès that he should apply to General Bonaparte: 'There's your man. He will carry out your *coup* much better than I could.'

Napoleon was also the popular favourite – the famous victor of the Italian campaign, and now the founder of an apparently successful colony in the East. When the time was ripe, he would take power as Sieyès' 'sword', but would keep it for himself. A few years later, he described his tactics:

> I was very careful. It was one of the periods of my life when I acted with the soundest judgement. I saw the Abbé Sieyès and promised him that his wordy Constitution would be put into effect. I received the leading Jacobin and Bourbon [royalist] agents. I listened to advice from everyone, but gave advice only in the interests of my own plans. I hid myself from the people, because I knew that when the moment came, curiosity to see me would bring them running after me. Everyone was caught in my nets and when I became head of state there was not a party in France that did not build some special hope on my success.
>
> From a conversation with Napoleon in 1803, recalled by Madame de Rémusat in her *Memoirs*; quoted in D.G. Wright, *Napoleon and Europe*, Longman, 1984.

However, the actual seizure of power was less smooth than this suggests. Most of the army would probably have supported Napoleon if he had simply taken over by force; but that would have created more conflicts and divisions in a country that was already bitterly divided – hardly a promising beginning for a warrior-leader who was determined to have a strong and united France behind him. Napoleon wanted, if possible, to present himself as the legitimate successor to the Directory, not as a military dictator. Even this course had its dangers, and actions that seem easy to spectators are viewed differently by those who put their lives at risk in carrying them out. Bourrienne, Napoleon's secretary, was on his way to St Cloud, just outside Paris, where the final scenes of the *coup* were enacted. He was accompanied by a friend, and

The Place Louis XV is now known as the Place de la Concorde. Can you think of some other events that 'success has legitimated', and that might now be viewed differently if they had failed?

> As we were passing through the Place Louis XV [used for executions] he asked me what was to be transacted, and what I thought of the events now at issue. 'My friend', said I, 'we shall either sleep in the Luxembourg Palace, or we finish here.' Who could have told which was to be the conclusion? Success has legitimated, as a noble enterprise, what the least circumstance would have converted into a criminal attempt.
>
> Fauvelet de Bourrienne, *Memoirs of Napoleon Bonaparte*, 1829.

And in fact the *coup* was nearly bungled, although it began well enough on 18 Brumaire (9 November). Two of the five Directors, Sieyès and Ducos, who were among the plotters, began the dismantling of the Directory by resigning. A third Director, Napoleon's one-time patron, Barras, was induced to quit by threats or bribery; the other two were put under temporary arrest. General Bonaparte was named as commander of the Paris garrison and the troops guarding the legislative bodies – that is, the 'parliament' of the Directory, consisting of the Council of the Ancients and the Council of the Five Hundred. But when these assemblies met at St Cloud on 19 Brumaire, Napoleon's speech to the Ancients was

Brumaire. Here the Bonaparte of heroic myth stands unmoved among a hostile crowd. In reality the coup was badly bungled and for a time Napoleon lost his nerve.

unconvincing; and when he moved on to the Jacobin-dominated Council of the Five Hundred he was denounced as a dictator and threatened with outlawry; the deputies rightly realized that the vaguely described dangers from which Napoleon claimed to be saving them were merely excuses to make them sign away their authority. Angry deputies crowded round him, and he was forced out of the hall, apparently paralysed with shock. His brother Lucien, who was serving as president of the Five Hundred, saved the day by using his authority to win over the parliamentary guards, who were told that a minority of the assembly were terrorizing the rest. Napoleon had accidentally scratched his own face during the fracas in the Council of the Five Hundred, and this was cited as evidence that some of the deputies were armed with daggers and had tried to assassinate him. Grenadiers were sent to drive out the Five Hundred at bayonet-point, the Ancients voted to replace the Directory with a provisional government consisting of Napoleon Bonaparte, Sieyès and Ducos, and later on Lucien collected a favourable minority of the scattered deputies who confirmed the changes in the names of the Council of the Five Hundred.

In a proclamation issued the same evening, Napoleon gave his version of events:

Intimidated, the agitators dispersed and went away. The majority, protected from their blows, came freely and peacefully back to the council room; propositions necessary to the safety of the public were heard. The . . . resolution which is to become the new and provisional law of the Republic was discussed and prepared.
Quoted in Tulard, *Napoleon: the myth of the saviour.*

Paris accepted the change quietly, and it became clear that the revolutionary impulse that had so often sent crowds on to the streets had spent itself. Napoleon was now at the centre of power.

Few people regretted the passing of the Directory at the time. Most

This gives the impression that Tulard himself isn't convinced. Think about what might have happened if Lucien had not been President of the Five Hundred and Napoleon had failed. With a certain amount of luck, even a very shaky regime may survive and consolidate.

historians have concluded that the regime was bound to fall, even if Napoleon's *coup* had failed. One historian, who emphasizes the achievements of the Directory, puts it this way:

Did the situation in which the Directory found itself make a *coup* necessary? All the Brumaire historians think so. There was no other way out.
Tulard, *Napoleon: the myth of the saviour.*

It was on this basis that Napoleon presented himself as the saviour of the Revolution.

The Revolution: saved or betrayed?

After Brumaire, Sieyès discovered the full strength of the 'sword' he had drawn. When a new constitution was devised Napoleon secured far more power than Sieyès had intended, being nominated head of the government as First Consul. Sieyès and Ducos retired, and two lesser figures, Cambacérès and Lebrun, replaced them in the three-man executive as Second and Third Consuls; but their powers were only advisory. The representative and consultative bodies (Senate, Legislative Assembly and Tribunate) did keep some independence, but soon enough Napoleon's unbroken successes in politics and war made his will irresistible. His dominant position in France was confirmed by his appointment as First Consul for life (1802), and finally by his assumption of the imperial title in May 1804.

None of this would have been possible without victories in the field that ended the threat from the Second Coalition. In May 1800 Napoleon made a daring Alpine descent into Lombardy by the St Bernard Pass, and broke the Austrian hold on Italy at the battle of Marengo. His reputation as a military genius was now universally recognized – though, paradoxically, Marengo was the closest-run of all his victories, hanging on the last-minute arrival of reinforcements on the battlefield.

To patriotic Frenchmen, Napoleon the soldier was the saviour of France. 'Napoleon appeared and put an end to the series of defeats to which we were

The inauguration of the Council of State, Napoleon's 'cabinet' at the beginning of the Consulate. The Roman salutes and the self-consciously 'heroic' attitudes make the picture uncannily suggestive of twentieth century totalitarianism.

exposed by the feeble government of the Directory', wrote the novelist Stendhal. But many of his contemporaries were even more impressed by Napoleon's domestic policy during the Consulate. To them, he was the man who healed the wounds inflicted by the Revolution, restored order, and brought back prosperity. Whether, in doing so, he betrayed or fulfilled the Revolution, has been keenly disputed ever since.

Napoleon's extraordinary energy is undeniable; at his peak he could work 18 hours at a stretch, concentrating fiercely on one subject after another, and tackling each with a notable lack of prejudices and fixed ideas. During the Consulate he was particularly successful in energizing his subordinates, who made significant contributions to the success of the new regime. French law, chaotic even before the Revolution, was made uniform and consolidated into the famous Code Napoléon. The irreconcilables among the Jacobins were suppressed, but the broader-based royalist movement was met with a clever mixture of force and conciliation that ended the long-smouldering revolts in the west and south of France. Much of the royalists' support among the peasants was cut away by the Concordat of 1802, an agreement between Napoleon and Pope Pius VII that ended the bitter antagonism between Church and State in revolutionary France; instead of inciting the faithful to support the royalists against the Republic, the Church now became a powerful ally of the First Consul. An amnesty was extended to the thousands of self-exiled royalist *émigrés*, many of whom had borne arms against the Republic; they were now welcome to return to France, provided they were prepared to accept the existing order. Here too, Napoleon's policy was successful, despite royalist grumbles and protests:

> Nearly all of them swore that it would be dishonourable to accept such an amnesty, but while the words were still on their lips they were making preparations to leave; those who had set out on the previous day were bitterly reproached by those who were going to follow them on the next.
> Written by a Frenchman in London; quoted in Louis Madelin, *The Consulate and the Empire*, Heinemann, 1934.

Finally, France became prosperous again under the Consulate. There may have been an element of good luck in this, since it can be argued that it was economic changes rather than government policy that ended the prolonged depression of the Directory period. But the Consulate certainly created the favourable climate that is recognized as of decisive importance for trade and industry. The establishment of a Bank of France and other economic measures restored faith in the currency, and the promise of social and political stability encouraged economic expansion.

The price of these benefits was liberty. Each new step towards dictatorship was submitted to the people, who approved it in a plebiscite. Napoleon was the first ruler to appreciate that this apparently ultra-democratic device actually favoured the government; his example was later followed by several leaders of the 'strong man' type who wanted to disguise the nature of their regimes.

Real power was increasingly concentrated in Napoleon's hands. Within a few years, the assemblies had become subservient. Police spies monitored public opinion and shadowed suspected malcontents. The press was kept under strict control, books were censored, and influential writers who refused to conform were exiled to the provinces. The Church, and the educational institutions set up by Napoleon's government, were used to make Frenchmen loyal and obedient subjects without ideas of their own.

There seems no doubt that Napoleon's policies were popular throughout

Before the Revolution, each region of France had its own laws, and there were all sorts of local exceptions and similar complications. A team of lawyers supervised by Napoleon produced a single code of laws that applied to the entire country – the Code Napoléon.

For details of the antagonism between Church and State, see p. 15.

In a plebiscite, or referendum, the voters are presented with a single issue. For example, they are asked to answer Yes or No to a question such as 'Should Napoleon Bonaparte be named Consul for life?' Can you think of a reason why a majority of people may be willing to vote for an opposition party in an election, but rarely reject the government recommendation in a plebiscite? You might like to investigate other rulers who have made frequent use of plebiscites, for example the Emperor Napoleon III, Adolf Hitler, and President de Gaulle of France.

The First Consul at Malmaison. In this painting by Isabey, Napoleon is still apparently the embodiment of republican virtue.

the Consulate and for some years afterwards. As often happens after a long period of turmoil, many people were prepared to sacrifice some, or all, of their liberties in return for peace and security; as Napoleon put it, 20 years later, 'everyone had had enough of the Revolution, of Assemblies, of unrest and of internal dissensions'. Members of most factions found that they could reconcile themselves to life under a new regime, although republicans were outraged by some of Napoleon's departures from the revolutionary tradition. The principle of equality was weakened by the creation of a new decoration, the Legion of Honour, which recognized achievement; its holders were given various ranks, so that they formed a pyramid or hierarchy, with Napoleon himself at the top. When his ex-Jacobin minister, Thibaudeau, objected that such decorations were mere toys, Napoleon remarked cynically that 'It is with toys that men are governed.' But even after becoming Emperor, his respect for the republican tradition remained strong enough for him to delay the creation of a new nobility until 1808.

Many republicans also disliked the Concordat. In their eyes, the Church stood for superstition and a blindly regressive conservatism. Napoleon had to force the measure through against considerable opposition from his own advisers and the otherwise accommodating legislative bodies. His own view was simply that national reconciliation was essential. Although his reputation stood high among Catholics as the man who had 'restored the altars', Napoleon himself had no religious beliefs. But he did regard religion as socially useful, since it strengthened the authority of the civil power and

France proclaiming Napoleon Emperor – a contemporary print in which the event is celebrated with romantic enthusiasm but adorned with such classical trappings as laurels, a triumphal chariot and various mythological females.

encouraged the poor man to accept his fate instead of cutting the rich man's throat: 'In religion I see not the mystery of the Incarnation but the mystery of the social order.'

The republican view was expressed by one of Napoleon's generals, Delmas, after the First Consul attended mass at Notre Dame: 'All that was missing was the million men who died to put an end to all that', he exclaimed in disgust. And when Napoleon was crowned emperor, in the presence of the Pope and with his blessing, Stendhal wrote that

Charlatanism: quackery – phoney solutions for human problems.

It was a blatant alliance of every form of charlatanism; religion coming forward to consecrate tyranny and making human happiness the pretext.
Quoted in Madelin, *The Consulate and the Empire.*

Nevertheless Thibaudeau, Delmas and Stendhal all made successful careers under the Empire, and this suggests that they did not believe it to be a total betrayal of the Revolution. Napoleon's own view was clear. He was proud of his policy of reconciliation:

By 'revolutionaries' Napoleon of course meant ex-revolutionaries who had accepted his regime.

The greatest seigneurs of the old regime dine with revolutionaries. My government has brought about this fusion.
Napoleon in conversation, December 1812; quoted in J. Hanoteau (ed.), *Memoirs of General Caulaincourt*, 1950.

And he repeatedly claimed to have consolidated the Revolution, and therefore to have brought it to an end – a very different thing from destroying it. A proclamation issued less than a month after Brumaire takes this line, asserting that the new constitution was

The slogan of the Revolution had been Liberty, Equality, Fraternity. By 1799 'fraternity' had become 'property'. Do you think there is any significance in the order in which the 'Sacred rights' are mentioned? Why should Napoleon be so insistent that 'the Revolution is over'?

. . . based upon the true principles of representative government, and on the sacred rights of property, equality and liberty. The powers it sets up will be strong and lasting. Citizens, the Revolution is stabilized on the principles which began it. The Revolution is over.
Proclamation of 15 December 1799, quoted in J.M. Thompson, *Napoleon Bonaparte: his rise and fall*, Blackwell, 1952.

One of Napoleon's outstanding British biographers agrees, going so far as to declare that

His greatest conquest was not Europe, but the French Revolution. His most lasting monument is not the Arc de Triomphe or the flags at the Invalides, but the laws and institutions in which he adapted the ideas of 1789 to the traditions of the monarchy, and enabled France to survive three invasions and a century and a half of political unrest.
J.M. Thompson, *Napoleon Bonaparte.*

The Invalides in Paris houses the Army Museum, which contains numerous French and captured flags from Napoleon's campaigns. How sound is the argument presented here? Is it self-evident that Napoleon's laws and institutions – rather than her strong sense of national identity, or her armies and allies – 'enabled France to survive'? And may not the laws and institutions even have *caused* or aggravated the political instability?

But even in their modified Brumairian form, as 'property, equality and liberty', the 'sacred rights' of the Revolution were decidedly *not* preserved and consolidated by Napoleon. Liberty was the most obvious casualty – and liberty was what many people believed the Revolution to have been about, in England and other countries, as well as in France. It was not just the abolition of privilege, but the positive boon of liberty, that made the poet Wordsworth recall the beginning of the Revolution as a time when

Bliss was it in that dawn to be alive,
But to be young was very Heaven!
From Book Eleven of William Wordsworth's great autobiographical poem, *The Prelude*, published (posthumously) in 1850.

Napoleon viewed the Revolution in quite a different light. He argued shrewdly that he had put aside Revolutionary *theories* but retained Revolutionary *interests* – that is, the legal and material gains made since 1789. Historians have tended to agree with this analysis, though without necessarily accepting his contemptuous dismissal of political liberty as 'theory'. However, a French historian, highly favourable to Napoleon, has claimed that

What does Madelin imply by 'in her heart of hearts'? Do you find anything to criticize in his use of the phrase?

. . . everything was reduced to the question of authority. But, in her heart of hearts, France had never asked for anything else . . . organized, coherent authority, just and firm.
Of the three goals at which the Revolution in its idealistic days had aimed – Liberty, Equality, and Fraternity – the people still remained fanatically faithful to one – Equality . . . . The destruction of privilege, equality before the law, equality of taxation, careers open to all alike, this was all they wanted, though they wanted it badly.
Madelin, *The Consulate and the Empire.*

'Careers open to talent' was one of the best-advertised advantages of Napoleon's regime, in which, it was said, a common soldier might hope to become a prince – by contrast with the old monarchical regime, which reserved the highest positions in the land for men of noble birth. But this is a very limited view of what 'equality' means. All Frenchmen may have been equal before the law, but the gap between rich and poor remained so wide that, in practice, people from different classes were far from equal, either materially or in terms of opportunities. This was, of course, true of the rest of Europe; but during the French Revolution there *had* been a strain of radicalism which on occasion led to government efforts to distribute resources more fairly. The Directory, not Napoleon, was responsible for the end of such efforts; nevertheless, an aspiration towards greater equality in a material sense was another aspect of the Revolution that was not 'consolidated' by the Consulate and Empire.

In reality, then, Napoleon preserved only those aspects of the Revolution that benefited certain groups and classes – exceptional or lucky individuals among the masses, a peasantry which had made substantial gains and had become conservative, and above all the propertied and influential people for whom the new legal and financial 'equality' was of real value. Many

For example, during the Revolution equality of the sexes was recognized and divorce was allowed on several grounds including incompatibility. The Code Napoléon subjected the wife to her husband and made divorce difficult to obtain. The (male) head of a household was legally entitled to imprison an adulterous wife or disobedient child!

historians regard these 'notables' – landowners, investors and office-holders – as the main beneficiaries of the Revolution, claiming that Napoleon acted as their champion and ruled by virtue of their support until his ambitions conflicted with their interests. It was above all these people who were prepared in 1799 to give up their political rights in return for undisturbed enjoyment of other benefits. Nor did they object to the provisions of the Napoleonic Code – which, though impressive, was in many respects reactionary; women, for example, lost most of the rights they had acquired during the Revolution, and were subjected to the authority of their fathers or husbands. So the 'equality' that Napoleon maintained and defended was of a very limited kind indeed; and if he *was* the legitimate heir of the Revolution, then the Revolution was a rather different kind of event from what most contemporaries believed it to be.

Peacemaker or warmonger?

One of Napoleon's most popular acts as First Consul was to bring about a general peace after France had been at war for almost ten years. Moreau's victory at Hohenlinden in Germany, following on Napoleon's reconquest of Italy, forced Austria to conclude the treaty of Lunéville (February 1801), which left France in control of all northern Italy, recognized the Rhine as her eastern frontier, and in effect made Napoleon the dominant figure in central Europe. Tsar Paul I was already friendly, since British interference with neutral shipping had angered Russia, Denmark and the other northern powers, who had formed a League of Armed Neutrality to oppose British pretensions. Only Britain herself carried on the war; but with dangerous discontent at home and no allies on the Continent, she too was ready to make peace. The British had something to offer – the island of Malta and a number of valuable colonies captured from France and her Dutch and Spanish allies. In the spring of 1802, Britain's position was strengthened by victory over the French in Egypt, Nelson's triumph over the Danes at the battle of Copenhagen, and the timely assassination of the pro-French Tsar, who was replaced by his son Alexander. These events no doubt persuaded Napoleon to open urgent negotiations, since the collapse of the League of Armed Neutrality left him with no prospect of damaging British trade by keeping her goods out of Europe. Peace probably also seemed desirable to end Britain's naval blockade of French ports, allowing a revival of France's navy and renewed colonial expansion. Since both sides were willing, preliminary terms were agreed in October 1801, and in March 1802 France and Britain signed the treaty of Amiens which ended hostilities.

A little over a year later the two countries were at war again; and they continued to be so until the fall of Napoleon in 1814. Britain found such allies as she could on the Continent, where the other major powers remained fundamentally hostile to the new France and its upstart ruler. Because the campaigns of 1805-7 and 1809 went in Napoleon's favour and led to the rapid growth of his empire, it is easy to assume that he was the aggressor against Austria, Prussia and Russia in these instances. But in fact he went to war because the other powers were visibly preparing to strike. One of the most famous of modern historians makes this interesting judgment:

Napoleon may well have aspired to found a great European empire. But all his wars except the last [against Russia] were preventive wars, provoked by the preparations that others were making to attack him.
A.J.P. Taylor, *How Wars Begin*, Hamish Hamilton, 1979.

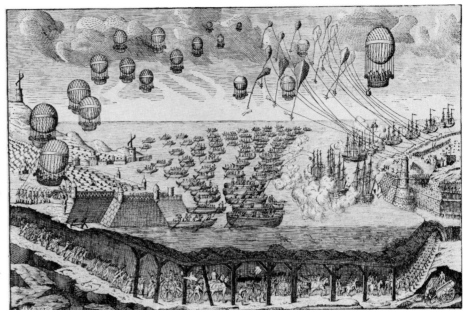

England invaded by sea, air and underground. This fantasy engraving of 1803 reflects French frustration at the protection offered to her ancient enemy by the Channel. In the event, Napoleon was only too glad of an excuse to abandon his camp at Boulogne and use 'the Army of England' on dry land at Ulm and Austerlitz.

English confidence in her security is conveyed in this cartoon of 1804, which compares Napoleon with Gulliver among the giants. The court looks on with interest at the Frenchman's futile maritime efforts.

But was Napoleon to blame right at the beginning, in 1803? If so, then it could be argued that all his wars stemmed from an initial act of bad faith and aggression. British historians have usually taken this view, although there have been some notable exceptions in recent years. The issue is a complicated one, since the period of growing Anglo-French antagonism in 1802-3 was marked by a flurry of offers and counter-offers, accusations and denials, that can be selectively arranged to make a case on one side or another. One way to cut through all the detail is to ask just what terms were agreed at Amiens, and whether they were carried out.

The main provisions were that (1) Britain would return all her colonial conquests except Trinidad (which had belonged to Spain) and Ceylon (previously Dutch); (2) the French would evacuate Naples and the Papal States, and in return (3) the British would hand back Malta, captured in 1801, to the Knights of St John, after which the neutrality of this strategically important island would be guaranteed by the great powers. The French did withdraw from southern Italy, but the British delayed their withdrawal from Malta and finally refused altogether to go. As far as the letter of the treaty is concerned, they were in the wrong, as Lord Castlereagh, later Foreign Secretary, tacitly admitted by remarking that 'It will be difficult to convince the world that we do not fight solely for Malta'. A.J.P. Taylor believes that the entire episode is revealing of British hypocrisy:

> What was the technical reason [for the outbreak of war]? The technical reason may not be why a war starts but it is at least the spark. The technical reason was simply this: that during the revolutionary war the Royal Navy occupied Malta. It was not theirs, it was not British . . . and one of the terms of the Peace of Amiens was that the British would give up Malta. When the time came they refused to do so. They said to Napoleon 'You have not withdrawn from certain territories you have occupied in Europe – therefore we are going to stay in Malta.' The British are entitled always to mistrust other people but others are not entitled to mistrust the British. That is why England . . . was known abroad as 'Perfide Albion', because the British have two standards, one for themselves and one for other people.
> Taylor, *How Wars Begin.*

'Perfide Albion' is French for 'Perfidious Albion', i.e. Treacherous England. Britain's reputation on the Continent was as a self-serving power, likely to let down her allies when it suited her; British historians, by contrast, have tended to treat such lapses with a sympathetic understanding less often extended to Britain's enemies. Hence Taylor's remarks about the British double standard.

Sphere of influence: the area in which a state's leadership is accepted, even though it does not directly control it. After Amiens, the French sphere of influence included Holland, Switzerland and northern Italy. Colonial powers have often avoided conflict by agreeing to divide disputed areas into two or more spheres of influence, as Britain and Russia did in 1907 in the case of Persia.

Do you think that this states the issue fairly? Work out your response *before* reading any further. See whether you agree with the author's comments – and don't be too hasty in accepting his point of view.

And in reality this was less of a tit-for-tat situation than Taylor implies, since the territories from which Napoleon failed to withdraw were not mentioned in the Peace of Amiens; it could be argued that he proceeded to violate the terms of the treaty of Lunéville, made between France and Austria, but *not* those of Amiens. The British complaint against Napoleon was not that he had broken the Peace of Amiens, but that he had violated its spirit, for example by imposing high tariffs to stop British goods from competing with French products in the French sphere of influence. The British position has been sympathetically summarized as follows:

> During the interval between the Preliminaries of London in October and the signing of the definitive Peace of Amiens in March 1802, all the unwritten expectations which had induced the Addington government to sign the Preliminaries would wither. Nothing had been said in the articles about commerce; nothing about the French boundaries recognized by the Peace of Lunéville; nothing about Piedmont, nor the independence of the satellite republics of Holland, Switzerland and Lombardy; nor about the reorganization of Germany, nor about Elba and Parma. There was nothing in these articles to restrain French colonial ambitions. In all these areas the British government found that it had been duped.
> Piers Mackesy, *War Without Victory: the downfall of Pitt, 1799-1802*, O.U.P., 1984.

This passage contains some ideas and implications that are well worth examining. For example, it assumes that Britain's 'unwritten expectations' should have been satisfied by Napoleon. But wouldn't most British governments and diplomats, placed in similar circumstances, insist that a treaty is no more and no less than the document signed by the parties concerned? That is basically the view a court of law would take of any kind of written contract. But even more curious is the fact, made clear in the passage just quoted, that Britain's supposed grievances were known *before* the signature of the definitive treaty: her 'unwritten expectations' had 'withered', but she made peace all the same; so disappointed expectations could not be a legitimate reason for not carrying out its provisions. Above all, it is hard to see how the British government can be described as having been 'duped'.

It seems more reasonable to suppose that Britain made peace because she saw no way of challenging France's dominant position on the Continent, and allowed a new war to break out when it suited her to do so. That is, like most nations at most times, she consulted her own interests. King George III described Amiens as 'an *experimental* peace', and Admiral Young expressed a widely held sense that the situation was unstable, but that Britain must bide her time:

With France as strong as she is now, Europe can never be secure; perhaps the great continental powers will be at length convinced of this and heartily join their forces to reduce her within reasonable bounds.
Quoted in Mackesy, *War Without Victory*.

One important factor in British decision-making may well have been the changing attitude of Russia, whose Tsar gradually took a more favourable view of the British possession of Malta and began to seem a likely ally. It is also possible that – without having been 'duped' – the British government failed to anticipate how rapidly French colonial ambitions would revive, and how little economic benefit Britain would derive from peace:

War had placed a great strain on the British economy, but peace with France seemed likely to impose an even greater burden . . . The peace of Lunéville presented France with an opportunity not only of securing allies in western Germany but also of opening markets to a France which might displace Britain as the dominant commercial power . . . The belief held generally in Britain that the signing of peace would lead to an expansion of British trade did not in fact prove correct . . . British trade . . . could make little impression upon areas of French influence . . . The progress of France in promoting her own trade was imposing . . . There was a growing conviction that Britain would be more prosperous if she resumed the war.
R.F. Leslie, *The Age of Transformation*, Blandford, 1964.

An acute contemporary comment on French and British imperialism: Napoleon and the British prime minister, William Pitt, carve up a plum-pudding globe between them.

By contrast, Napoleon did not want war in 1803, as even most hostile historians are willing to concede: he was intent on the consolidation of his regime at home and the imminent reorganization of western Germany into a French-protected confederation. In that case, it can be argued that he should have gone beyond the letter of the treaty and taken a more conciliatory attitude towards the British; but that is to say that he may have made serious mistakes, not that he was to blame for the renewal of the war. Whether or not he would have 'shown his true colours' by committing some overt aggression if the peace had lasted longer, can only be a matter of speculation.

None of this need make us idealize Napoleon, who in many respects was undeniably ruthless, unscrupulous and avid for power. Certainly we need not be convinced by his own often-expressed regrets, which must inevitably be suspected of a propagandist motive:

> Napoleon said this on St Helena, where he deliberately tried to put the history of his reign in the most favourable light. We must not take his word for his good intentions, but neither can we assume without evidence that they were non-existent.

At Amiens I believed in all good faith that my own fate and that of France were settled. I was going to devote myself entirely to the administration of the country and I believe that I should have done wonders.
Quoted in Madelin, *The Consulate and the Empire*.

But, whether or not we accept this, it does seem that the conventional account of Napoleon as an out-and-out militarist is by no means unchallengeable. There is a good deal of evidence that Napoleon, like the British, regarded conflict as inevitable – conflict with the British as commercial rivals, and conflict with the European powers because of their hostility to the Revolution and its imperial successor-state:

The First Consul: Now tell me: do you believe that these governments who have just signed peace with us will still remain our enemies?
State Counsellor: I find it hard to think otherwise.
First Consul: Then we must draw the consequences . . . it is better for us if we fight sooner rather than later. For every day that passes weakens the memory they have of their own recent defeats and diminishes the prestige which our own latest victories give us.
A conversation of 1802, recorded in Thibaudeau's *Memoirs*; quoted in Maurice Hutt, *Napoleon*, Prentice Hall, 1972.

Although Napoleon did not act on this conviction at once, its existence is of some significance. This aspect of his wars – the clash of incompatible regimes – will be examined again, from a slightly different angle, on page 46-48.

Master of Europe

The art of war

Following in the wake of his famous Italian campaigns, Napoleon's triumphs of 1805-7 convinced many of his contemporaries that he was an invincible military genius, fully the equal of Alexander the Great and Julius Caesar. In September 1805, when Austria and Russia marched against him, he led his forces into the heart of Germany at lightning speed, crossed the Danube and enveloped an Austrian army at Ulm, compelling its bewildered and demoralized commander, General Mack, to surrender without offering battle (20 October). Five weeks later, faced with the main, numerically superior Austro-Russian army, Napoleon lured the allies to

The cult of military glory: a laurel-wreathed Napoleon distributes the eagles to his wildly enthusiastic army. Painting by J.L. David, the most distinguished artist employed to further Napoleon's glory.

Austerlitz and tempted them to overextend themselves by exploiting apparent weaknesses in the French position; then, with a carefully prepared counter-stroke, the French stormed the depleted enemy centre on the heights of Pratzen, breaking the opposing host in two and routing it with heavy casualties. The Russians retreated into Poland, leaving their Austrian allies to sue for peace; the subsequent treaty, signed at Pressburg (December 1805), involved considerable sacrifices of territory to Napoleon and his German allies, Bavaria and Württemburg.

Although Austerlitz (2 December 1805) remained Napoleon's most famous victory, the war of 1806-7 against Prussia was even more overwhelmingly successful in its outcome. The indecisive King of Prussia, Frederick William III, had intended to join the Austro-Russian alliance, but had hesitated long enough to hear of Napoleon's victory at Austerlitz, which acted as a deterrent. But, urged on by his wife, Queen Louise, and his overconfident generals, he made a secret agreement with Russia, and in September 1806 invaded the territory of France's Saxon allies. Napoleon again reacted with great speed; he was determined to smash the Prussians before the Russians arrived to help them. On 14 October, having concentrated most of his forces at Jena, Napoleon destroyed one Prussian army, which he mistakenly believed to be the main body of the enemy; but on the same day, at Auerstädt, one of his best generals, Davout, performed the still more impressive feat of overthrowing the major Prussian force, which outnumbered his 27,000 men by over two to one. The French

Austerlitz, the most famous of all Napoleonic victories.

pursued their defeated enemies relentlessly, and as Prussian morale collapsed, armies and fortresses surrendered one after another and Davout's troops marched into the Prussian capital, Berlin.

Frederick William fled with the remnants of his forces to the safety of the Russian army, which bore the brunt of the ensuing battles. In East Prussia (now northern Poland), where the roads were bad and the winter weather atrocious, Napoleon received his first check: at Eylau, fought partly in a snowstorm, the French were heavily outnumbered for most of the day (8 February 1807) and suffered far higher casualties than they were used to – perhaps 20,000 men to the Russians' 15,000. The French held the field, so that both sides had some justification for claiming a victory; but it was clear that, for once, Napoleon had not thoroughly discomfited his opponents. However, when the two sides emerged from winter quarters, the French quickly seized the initiative. Danzig (modern Gdańsk) was besieged and captured. The Russians under Benningsen were forced back and outmanoeuvred; then, on 14 June 1807, their main force was caught at Friedland, divided and with its back to the River Alle. They were driven back with terrible losses (including 80 of their 130 cannon) and pursued as far as the River Niemen until the Tsar requested an armistice. At Tilsit, on a raft in the middle of the Niemen, Napoleon and Alexander I had a celebrated meeting which resulted in a complete reversal of alliance. To all appearances, the Tsar was entirely won over by Napoleon. Russia and France became partners; Alexander recognized all the dynastic and territorial changes in Europe decreed by the French Emperor; and Russia joined the 'Continental System' of economic warfare, through which he hoped to defeat Britain. There could now be no doubt that Napoleon dominated the entire European continent.

French imperial propaganda elaborated the image of Napoleon as a superman, winning his victories through sheer genius for war. And certainly few writers have denied him genius, however much they have disapproved of what he did with it. Apart from his phenomenal powers of work – never more obsessively applied than during the course of a campaign – he had the great leader's flair for sustaining his troops' morale and inspiring them to exceptional efforts. He created an illusion of intimacy by his wanderings round the campfires on the night before a battle, and by the way in which he allowed the soldiers to talk back familiarly to him. He was famous for recognizing individuals in the ranks who had fought with him in previous campaigns (a feat that has often been copied, since it is in fact quite simple to perform with the help of a little preliminary research!). Parades and reviews kept the army alert, and proclamations and bulletins maintained its good opinion of itself. And soldiers, like many civilians, responded to the Roman-style symbols – such as the eagle standards – with which Napoleon glamorized his career of imperial conquest.

This was a style of leadership unknown to the aristocratic military

One exception is the Russian novelist Leo Tolstoy (1828-1910), who was refreshingly sceptical about the very notion of 'military genius'. His Napoleonic epic *War and Peace* is immensely long but very readable – and one of the world's great stories.

Genius on the field of battle: a compelling image of Napoleon at Jena.

tradition of Europe, and all the more effective when practised by a man of Napoleon's personal magnetism and enormous energy. Thanks to these, and his overmastering impulse to dominate, the French army never suffered from divided counsels. Napoleon's will drove the entire military machine. As the active head of both the nation and the army he took every major decision and many minor ones, and was able to ensure that the full resources of the state were employed to support each campaign. It was an astonishing and impressive state of affairs, though its dependence on one man's physical and mental health made it also a potentially vulnerable one.

The campaigns were also unlike anything that Europeans had experienced. What most astonished Napoleon's adversaries was the speed and flexibility with which his operations were conducted. His forces appeared in the theatre of war long before they were expected, and proceeded to combine, disperse, feint, turn, break off, change direction and strike home in a fashion that seemed miraculous. Initially, other European armies were not like this. They were tightly disciplined bodies of men who marched slowly, in parade-ground fashion, encumbered by heavy baggage-trains carrying equipment and provisions, as well as by powder magazines and siege-guns. They conducted long-drawn-out sieges or, after stately manoeuvres, fought set-piece battles. Confronted by Napoleon's tactics, their commanders were liable to become indignant at French unorthodoxy; during the first Italian campaign, an officer is said to have complained that 'They sent a young madman who attacks right, left and from the rear. It's an intolerable way of making war.'

But even the greatest military genius cannot succeed without effective instruments; and Napoleon was fortunate in the army and the mode of warfare that he took over from his predecessors. French troops were able to travel fast because they travelled light, shouldering packs that weighed about an eighth of those borne by Prussian foot-soldiers. This was mainly because, instead of carrying their provisions with them, they lived off the country, requisitioning everything they needed. It was not Napoleon who originated this practice, but the military experts of the Ancien Régime, whose books Napoleon read and profited from. In his *Essay on Tactics* one of these experts, J.A.H. Guibert, accurately described the new kind of warfare that would result:

Requisition: take over temporarily for military purposes, with or without the owner's consent.

The enemy must see me march when he believes me shackled by calculations of subsistence; this new type of war must astonish him, leave him no time to draw breath anywhere.
Quoted in Correlli Barnett, *Bonaparte*, Allen and Unwin, 1978.

Another French military man, Gribeauval, provided many of the technical means, by producing lighter, more mobile cannon with interchangeable parts. As a result, sheer speed often played a decisive role in Napoleon's campaigns; after Ulm, for example, he wrote to his wife, Josephine, 'I have destroyed the Austrian army by simple marching.'

Guibert's recommendation that 'War must feed on war' was first put into practice by the French Revolutionary armies – of necessity, since the revolutionary governments could not afford to feed them. The Revolution also produced the kind of common soldier most suited to the new warfare, which was a man with fighting spirit and a degree of initiative. The average soldier of the Ancien Régime was a criminal, a ne'er-do-well or a pressed man who served against his will. He could never be trusted and was likely to desert as soon as things became difficult. So armies *had* to be kept together, constantly supervised and savagely disciplined by an officer class

A pressed man: a soldier or sailor recruited by force.

drawn exclusively from the aristocracy. By contrast, the volunteer or conscript in the Revolutionary armies was not a subject, but a citizen. He believed in the cause for which he fought, or was at least inspired by patriotism. He could be trusted to forage without deserting, to march long distances and, arriving at the battlefield, to attack with enthusiasm – qualities which, as we have seen, Napoleon did everything in his power to encourage. Whereas the British soldier was flogged into obedience, the Frenchman served a government which had abolished corporal punishment. And, on a material plane, the Frenchman had more to hope for than his equivalent in other armies: he had a real chance of winning promotion, since the Revolution had abolished the aristocratic monopoly, and he had the freedom of action essential for successful looting.

In certain respects, then, Napoleon found a ready-made instrument – one that others could sometimes use with effect, as demonstrated by Moreau at Hohenlinden and Davout at Auerstädt. Furthermore, Napoleon contributed little to military theory and was surprisingly indifferent to innovations such as the early form of submarine devised by the American Robert Fulton. But his use of his instruments, and his execution of others' theories, were of the highest order – and he himself remarked that 'in war, execution is everything'. He had a superb eye for strategic and tactical advantage, seizing the briefest of opportunities for devastating strokes and counter-strokes. These were not always the reactions of a moment, but the result of grindingly hard work and intelligent anticipation. As a leading military historian points out,

Utilizing his great mental powers, he was in the habit of thinking through any military problem days, even months, in advance . . . . He invariably thought a problem through to the very bottom and examined it from every side, taking every foreseeable possibility into account and making allowances for every conceivable complication. Even then he was not satisfied, but must leave some space for pure chance . . . Thus most of his seemingly inspirational and opportunist adjustment of plans in mid-campaign were in fact preconsidered concepts, and it was rare for a situation to find him completely at a loss.
Chandler, *Napoleon*.

Napoleon's own view: 'What is luck? The ability to exploit accidents.

Thanks to this kind of planning, Napoleon was prepared for any situation that might arise; and his forces were organized accordingly, so that they could respond to events with the greatest possible flexibility. On the march, they were divided into a number of army corps, each of which followed a separate route. Among other things, this dispersal made it possible for tens of thousands of men to live off the country-side, which could not have supported a more concentrated force. In ordinary circumstances, dispersed forces would be vulnerable to attacks by the enemy army, which could overwhelm one scattered unit after another. However, the corps were organized to prevent that: each was a complete miniature army of up to 30,000 men, with infantry, cavalry, artillery and other units. Napoleon himself explained the advantages of the corps in a letter to his stepson Eugène:

Eugène Beauharnais was the son of Napoleon's first wife, Josephine. Eugène served as Napoleon's Viceroy in Italy, and commanded an army corps in the 1812 Russian campaign.

Here is the general principle of war – a corps of 25,000-30,000 men can be left on its own. Well handled, it can fight or alternatively avoid action, and manoeuvre according to circumstances without any harm coming to it, because an opponent cannot force it to accept an engagement, but if it chooses to do so it can fight alone for a long time. A division of 9000-17,000 men can be left for an hour on its own without inconvenience; it will contain a foe several times more numerous than itself, and will win time for the arrival of the army.
Quoted in Chandler, *Napoleon*.

Napoleon at Wagram, the last of his battles to bring about a victorious peace settlement.

Napoleon's final sentence offers a clue to his basic technique as a general. His army advanced rapidly through hostile territory, dispersed into corps so that it formed a 'net' in which the enemy could be 'caught' – that is, accurately located. By contrast, the opposing commander would know that his forces had made contact with a single corps, but might still have no idea where the rest of the French army was. If the situation seemed favourable from the French point of view, the corps would stand its ground in order to 'win time for the arrival of the army'. This was the critical moment, and the ability to concentrate his forces rapidly was the key to Napoleon's greatest successes. Military men have long recognized that overall superiority in numbers and firepower is less important than local superiority – the ability to bring overwhelming force to bear on the field of battle or in some vital sector. Napoleon was equally emphatic:

The art of war consists in having, with an inferior army, a force always greater than the enemy's on the point to be attacked, or on the point which is attacked. But this art is learned neither from books nor by practice. It is a tact of conduct which properly constitutes genius in war.
From a propagandist note dictated in 1797 to Bourrienne; quoted in his *Memoirs of Napoleon Bonaparte.*

Napoleon's distinctive technique of dispersal and concentration required meticulous planning in depth and careful thinking through. He excelled at both, but could never eliminate the unavoidable element of risk involved in dispersal. Some of his best victories, notably Marengo, were snatched from the jaws of disaster by the last-minute arrival of fresh troops who turned the battle in favour of the French.

In 1807 this seemed a relatively minor consideration. The French army appeared to be unbeatable, and the French Emperor, still a young man, was at the height of his powers. The potential weaknesses of Napoleonic warfare were yet to be revealed.

The dictatorship: temporary or permanent?

No one seriously doubts that Napoleon was a dictator. He never sought to deny the fact, though he did try to justify it in various ways. One was to claim that a concentration of personal power was unavoidable in the circumstances

... of the period preceding Brumaire, when our internal dissolution was complete, foreign invasion certain, and the destruction of the French inevitable ... From the

From Count de Las Cases' *Mémorial de Ste Helena Hélène* (1823), a journal recording Napoleon's conversation during the first year of his exile; it contains some of the fallen emperor's most effective self-justifications. This passage, with its account of the situation in 1797 and its sly use of phrases such as 'we decided', is well worth analyzing.

moment when we decided on the concentration of power, which alone could save us; when we determined on the unity of doctrines and resources which rendered us a mighty nation, the destinies of France depended solely on the character, the measures, and the principles of him who had been invested with this accidental dictatorship: from that moment the public interest, *the State, was myself*.
Quoted in Hutt, *Napoleon*.

The hostility of the great European powers, and the life-and-death struggle with Britain, made the continuation of the dictatorship inevitable, Napoleon claimed. This is a tenable (though by no means unchallengeable) view. But on occasion Napoleon went further, asserting that his dictatorship was essentially an interim measure that would have ended once the security of France was assured: 'If I had won in 1812, my constitutional reign would have begun!'.

All the evidence contradicts this declaration of intentions. With the years, Napoleon grew more, not less, autocratic. He insisted on total obedience, even from the members of his family who had supposedly become independent sovereigns. He constantly emphasized the importance of strong government, and his use of words such as 'mastery' is particularly revealing. For example, this passage from a letter dated 14 March 1814 to his older brother, Joseph, was written when his regime was on the point of collapse:

I will be master *everywhere* in France, as long as I have a breath in my body. Your character is quite different from mine. You like flattering people, and falling in with their ideas: I like people to please me, and to fall in with mine. I am master today, every bit as much as at Austerlitz.
Quoted in Thompson, *Napoleon's Letters*.

Over the years, a string of successes made Napoleon increasingly arrogant and certain of his own judgment. Like many other dictators, he found it more and more difficult to tolerate even 'loyal' opposition, and his two ablest ministers, Talleyrand and Joseph Fouché, were relieved of office in 1809-10. They were replaced by obedient routiners of the sort that Napoleon had come to prefer. His attitude seriously weakened the regime, which more than ever depended on the survival of a single man. Napoleon was to discover this for himself in 1812, during his absence in Russia, when a rumour of his death brought about a paralysis of the entire governmental machine that almost enabled a handful of conspirators to overthrow the Empire.

The Malet conspiracy. Led by an insane republican general, it ought to have posed no threat to a powerful and (so far) unbrokenly successful regime.

As well as more autocratic, Napoleon grew more conservative. In 1808 he created his own nobility, although the republican tradition remained

Procession on the day of Napoleon's marriage to the Austrian princess Marie-Louise in 1810. Though 'a child of the Revolution', Napoleon came to have a misplaced confidence in the value of old-fashioned dynastic alliances.

For example, Napoleon's crafty foreign minister, Talleyrand, became Prince of Benevento; Marshal Davout was created Prince of Eckmühl; and Marshal Ney became Prince of the Moskowa.

strong enough to influence the kind of titles that he chose: if a place-name was attached to a title, it was always a foreign one, suggestive of conquest rather than lordship over other Frenchmen. The Bonapartes became a family of kings and princes, ruling over large areas of Europe. And after the defeat of Austria in 1809, Napoleon divorced Josephine (who had failed to produce an heir) and married the Austrian princess Marie-Louise. Thus he joined the family circle of European sovereigns, evidently hoping to achieve a measure of international respectability. Once he even claimed that other monarchs should be grateful to him as the man who had 'tamed' the Revolution!

Later on, Napoleon realized that the Austrian marriage had been a mistake. It had seriously alarmed sections of French opinion, which had begun to fear that the revolutionary tradition was being betrayed, without seriously softening the hostility of the European powers. No doubt Europe's rulers were reactionaries who scorned Napoleon as an 'upstart soldier' and 'the revolution on horseback'; but by 1810 they also had good reasons for feeling insecure. Although it can be argued that most of Napoleon's major wars were preventive, the way he used the power that victory gave him certainly suggested that he was an incurable disturber of the peace, insatiably ambitious for himself and his family. The map was constantly redrawn, states were made and unmade, rulers unseated or transferred.

Napoleon and his family. This admiring later-nineteenth-century group portrait includes both of the dead emperor's wives and his son by Marie-Louise, the Duke of Reichstadt and former King of Rome (no. 4), who died at the age of 21.

Already irritated by Napoleon's tight control over the French Church, Pius refused to accept the Emperor's assumption that the Papal States must be part of his Continental System. The result was the French annexation of the Papal States and the imprisonment of Pius at Fontainebleu until the decline of Napoleon's fortunes made the quarrel between them irrelevant.

Indemnity: sum paid in compensation – at the end of a war, paid by the defeated to their conquerors, who are able to impose their view of the 'war-guilt' involved.

The sense of instability created by this was probably more important than occasional treaty violations by the French, which undoubtedly occurred but were arguably no worse than instances on the other side (for example by the British navy). Napoleon's quarrels with the Pope and the French occupation of the Papal States in February 1808, followed within weeks by the seizure of the Spanish throne, were further shocks. Napoleon was himself to admit that 'the immorality was too patent' in the way in which he played the Spanish king and his son off against each other, finally 'persuading' both to resign their rights. More significant even than the immorality was the fact that Napoleon had simply swept aside a historic dynasty (and one that was, however uncertainly, a French ally). After this, any European sovereign might justifiably have felt that his throne was not safe while Napoleon reigned.

The French occupation of Spain also proved to be a serious mistake from the military and political points of view. The fierce Spanish resistance and the embarrassing capitulation of 20,000 French troops at Baylen gave new heart to Napoleon's opponents in Europe. They also made war less popular in France. To French taxpayers, an important advantage of Napoleonic warfare was that it was self-supporting: the troops lived off the (foreign) land, and other expenses were more than met by the large indemnities paid by the defeated powers. But Spain was too poor to support the 350,000 French soldiers that were eventually stationed there in a vain effort to suppress the Spanish guerrillas and defeat the British expeditionary force in the peninsula – another unfortunate result of Napoleon's overweening ambition. Savage atrocities and reprisals, characteristic of the Spanish war, made it particularly unattractive to Frenchmen and accentuated the war-weariness that was beginning to surface among the working class. Fouché, his Minister of Police, warned him that

The working class evinces a strong dissatisfaction with conscription. In areas where they live, sealed papers have been delivered which contain provocative manuscripts against the government, addressed to girls, women, everyone.
Report dated 11 September 1808; quoted in Tulard, *Napoleon: the myth of the saviour.*

However, despite the warning signs, Napoleon emerged triumphant from the crises of 1808-9. He took command in Spain, defeated the British and reconquered most of the peninsula before he was forced to break off and return to face a resurgent Austria. The ensuing campaign, though presenting unexpected difficulties, was brought to a satisfying conclusion with a big victory at Wagram. A British landing at Walcheren in Holland was a humiliating failure, the anti-French revolts in Germany and the Tyrol collapsed, and Austria was converted into an ally through Napoleon's marriage to Marie-Louise. In March 1811 the birth of a son, to whom Napoleon gave the title 'King of Rome', appeared to crown his good fortune.

Nor was there any weakening of his grip in France, for Napoleon was the most watchful of despots. Although his employment of mediocrities made it unlikely that any serious rival would emerge from inside his administration, the Emperor never risked staying away from the capital for long. Even while campaigning he continued to supervise the operations of an empire that stretched from the Atlantic to Poland and Yugoslavia. Censorship of the press, book publishing and the theatre prevented criticism of the regime, and positive attempts were made to mould opinion through the educational system, the teachings of the Church and a steady stream of government propaganda and slanted war news. However,

Napoleon's shrewdest stroke was to insist that, whatever the economic situation, Parisians must be supplied regularly with bread. Breakdowns in food supplies to the capital had sparked many of the popular unheavals that had destroyed the monarchy and affected the course of the French Revolution; Napoleon's foresight was probably the main reason why Paris remained quiet throughout his reign. In this, as in many other respects, it must be admitted that his political acumen was remarkable, whether or not one approves of its objectives.

Master of Europe – in whose interest?

When attempting to justify his dictatorship Napoleon often claimed that it had benefited his entire empire, not just France. Among other advantages, French rule generally meant the introduction of the institutions associated with the Revolution. Napoleon himself made out the case in a document whose sincerity can hardly be questioned, since it was written to instruct his brother Jérôme on how to carry out his new duties as king of newly created Westphalia. There was to be no doubt as to who was master: with the letter Napoleon sent the constitution of the new kingdom, telling Jérôme that he must faithfully observe it. But the reasons Napoleon gives are interesting:

I am concerned for the happiness of your subjects, not only as it affects your reputation, and my own, but also for its influence on the whole European situation. Don't listen to those who say that your subjects are so accustomed to slavery that they will feel no gratitude for the benefits you give them. There is more intelligence in the Kingdom of Westphalia than they would have you believe; and your throne will never be firmly established except upon the trust and affection of the common people. What German opinion impatiently demands is that men of no rank, but of marked ability, shall have an equal claim upon your favour and your employment, and that every trace of serfdom, or of a feudal hierarchy between the sovereign and the lowest class of his subjects, shall be done away with. The benefits of the Code Napoléon, public trial, and the introduction of juries, will be the leading features of your Government. And to tell you the truth, I count more upon their effects, for the extension and consolidation of your rule, than upon the most resounding victories. I want your subjects to enjoy a degree of liberty, equality, and prosperity hitherto unknown to the German people. I want this liberal regime to produce, one way or another, changes which will be of the utmost benefit to the system of the Confederation, and to the strength of your monarchy . . . What people will want to return under the arbitrary Prussian rule, once it has tasted the benefits of a wise and liberal administration? In Germany, as in France, Italy, and Spain, people long for equality and liberalism. I have been managing the affairs of Europe long enough now to know that the burden of the privileged classes was resented everywhere. Rule constitutionally. Even if reason, and the enlightenment of the age, were not sufficient cause, it would be good policy for one in your position; and you will find that the backing of public opinion gives you a great natural advantage over the absolute kings who are your neighbours.
Dated 15 November 1807; quoted in Thompson, *Napoleon's Letters.*

The Confederation of the Rhine. See p. 16.

This is an impressive statement – all the more so because the liberalism professed by Napoleon is grounded in hard-headed political calculation. It gives credibility to various other remarks made by him ('my son will have to rule differently') which imply that he believed the future to lie with liberal, constitutional forms of government. In this sense it may be true that he regarded his dictatorship as an interim measure, though one that would (conveniently) last until his death. Whether, as he later claimed, his vision extended to a happily united Europe, must be a matter of speculation.

At first, the benefits of French rule were widely appreciated in states where commerce was becoming more important, for it was the middle class that stood to gain most from the abolition of privilege and the career open to talents. One of Napoleon's most serious mistakes was to imagine that the tiny Spanish middle class represented the outlook of the people at large; whereas even the most enlightened French-inspired reforms were detested as assaults on the traditional Spanish way of life. In time, however, most of the other non-French populations of the Empire also grew restive under Napoleon's rule.

This was partly – but only partly – because they resented foreign domination. Economic grievances were at least as important, and played a considerable part in kindling a new, nationalistic mood among the subject peoples. Everywhere in Europe, conquest had inevitably been followed by French economic penetration, so that French trade and manufactures largely replaced those of Britain. This situation was formalized by the Berlin and Milan decrees of 1806-7, which set up the Continental System and aimed to exclude all British goods from the Continent.

Since Britain was a great industrial and commercial power, Napoleon hoped to bring her to her knees by destroying the foundation of her greatness – her trade. In justification he could plead that the Continental System was no more than a response to Britain's naval blockade of the Continent. Furthermore, after Nelson's decisive victory at Trafalgar there was no other way that France could strike at a state that had shown itself implacably hostile to France. The 'Common Market' created by Napoleon was ultimately (in this interpretation) for the benefit of all; and if France benefited economically – well, wasn't France taking the brunt of the struggle against the common enemy? As King of Italy, Napoleon spelled out the consequences to his stepson and viceroy, Eugène:

All the raw silk from the Kingdom of Italy goes to England, [although it is supposedly bound for Germany] for there are no silk factories in Germany. It is therefore quite natural that I should wish to divert it from this route to the advantage of my French manufacturers . . . My principle is: France first. You must never lose sight of the fact that, if English commerce is supreme on the high seas, it is due to her sea power: it is therefore to be expected that, as France is the strongest land power, she should claim commercial supremacy on the Continent: it is indeed our only hope . . . it would be shortsighted not to recognize that Italy owes her independence to France; that it was won with French blood and French victories; that it must not be misused; and that nothing could be more unreasonable than to start calculating what commercial advantages France gets out of it . . . It is no use for Italy to make plans that leave French prosperity out of account; she must face the fact that the interests of the two countries hang together. Above all, she must be careful not to give France any reason for annexing her; for if it paid France to do this, who could stop her? So make this your motto too: France first.

Napoleon as overlord of Europe, receiving the Austrian envoy at the Congress of Erfurt in 1808. Here he was at the very height of his power and splendour, surrounded by satellite princes.

If I were to lose a great battle, a million men – nay, two million men of my old France would flock to my banners, and every purse in the country would be opened for me; but my Kingdom of Italy would desert me. I find it odd, then, that there should be any unwillingness to help the French manufacturers in what is only another way of damaging the English.

From a letter dated 23 August 1810; quoted in Thompson, *Napoleon's Letters*.

Whatever the merits of this viewpoint, it can hardly have pleased the silk producers of Italy, whose exports declined sharply, or many similar groups. Among the hardest hit were the Dutch, whose prosperity was almost entirely dependent on maritime trade – so much so that their sovereign, Napoleon's brother Louis, winked at many violations of the Continental System until the enraged Emperor forced Louis to abdicate and incorporated Holland in the French state (1810). Furthermore, consumers and businessmen almost everywhere in the French Empire suffered because of the Continental System, since France was nowhere near as economically advanced as Britain, and simply could not supply the European demand for textiles and other goods. As a result, smuggling became widespread, and the repressive counter-measures taken by Napoleon's officials brought home the autocratic nature of the regime in a way that remotely 'historic' events often failed to do.

Napoleon realized what was happening, but as late as December 1812 he remained confident that everything would come right in the end. To Caulaincourt, one of the few men who dared to criticize his policies,

He remarked that particular interests might here and there have been disturbed by police measures, or by combinations of circumstances which had nothing to do with the end he had in view. The people, however, were too enlightened, he said, not to see . . . that our laws, under which they now lived, offered real guarantees to every citizen against all arbitrary action . . . He went on to say: 'They were wrong to complain. It is the checks on trade that irk them. But those depend on considerations of a higher order, to which the interests of France must also yield. Only peace with England can end those inconveniences and their complaints. They need only be patient . . . England will be forced to conclude a peace consistent with the commercial rights of all nations. Then they will forget the inconveniences they complain of, while the consequent prosperity . . . will for the most part provide means for the prompt repair of all their losses . . .

It is said . . . that I abuse my power. I admit it, but I do it for the good of the Continent at large.'

From J. Hanoteau (ed.), *Memoirs of General Caulaincourt.*

Remarkably, this conversation took place after the disaster in Russia.

Napoleon's confidence proved misplaced. The Continental System disrupted the economic life of the Continent and made the imperial regime unpopular, but failed to break Britain's resistance. At the best of times Napoleon was forced to grant certain exemptions from his own decrees, and it was an embarrassing fact that the uniforms of the French army were made up from English cloth! Since the exemptions were always granted to French manufacturers, other Europeans were strengthened in their conviction that the Empire was in essence no more than a system of political domination and economic exploitation.

But it is easy to be wise after the event. We should judge the situation quite differently if Britain had been forced to ask for peace terms in 1811, when the Continental System was damaging the economy and unemployed workers were rioting. Even now, historians differ from one another on just how close to the edge Britain was. And it was not economic failure but military defeats that brought down the Empire.

However, Napoleon's ultimately disastrous policy of expansion was also

Unlike the relatively civilized conflicts elsewhere in Europe, the war in Spain was a savage business, with atrocities committed on both sides. In this famous painting by the Spanish artist Goya, The Third of May 1808, *a French firing squad deals with Spaniards who had opposed the occupation of Madrid.*

linked with the economic warfare he waged against Britain. If this was to succeed, every point of entry for British goods had to be closed. It was this consideration that led to the French involvement with Portugal and Spain (which is not to say that Napoleon did not *also* have the political man's urge constantly to increase his power at other people's expense). In a letter to his brother Louis, Napoleon summed up his policy in a sentence:

In this communication, dated 27 March 1808, Napoleon offered Louis the throne. Louis, wisely, declined.

Convinced as I am that I shall never secure lasting peace with England until I set the whole of Europe in motion, I have determined to put a French prince on the throne of Spain.
Quoted in Thompson, *Napoleon's Letters.*

Despite the negative results in Spain, Napoleon persisted in trying to stop other leaks in the Continental System. Holland was brought into line by annexation, and when it seemed necessary to seal up the Baltic, Napoleon did not hesitate to dethrone the Duke of Oldenburg, brother-in-law of France's ally, the Tsar of Russia. This was only one of many causes of friction between Napoleon and Alexander; but the most important was the fact that, contrary to the agreement made between the two emperors, Russia was importing quantities of British goods. If, as seems likely, this was the main reason for Napoleon's disastrous decision to attack his former ally, it can indeed be said that the Continental System ruined him.

Annexation: the act of taking permanent and complete control of a territory. Napoleon annexed Holland (which became a French province) because *indirect* control through his brother had proved inadequate.

Decline and Fall

The Russian disaster

See p. 42ff.

Even allowing for the hidden weaknesses of Napoleon's empire, its collapse was astonishingly swift and sudden. The French Emperor invaded Russia in 1812 with an army numbering over half a million men which was almost completely destroyed. In 1813, despite his still great resources, Napoleon was driven back across Europe to the French border; and in April 1814, with an allied army occupying Paris and Wellington marching up out of Spain from the south, Napoleon abdicated.

Napoleon's first really disastrous decision – to invade Russia – has often been criticized. Yet it was a logical one from his point of view, since only force would persuade the Tsar to reimpose the boycott on British goods. Napoleon may or may not have been right in believing that the Continental

The Tsar knew from experience that the boycott had ruinous effects on Russian trade.

System could defeat Britain, and he certainly underestimated its negative aspects. But his decision was not just an expression of will to power – though he was no doubt glad of an opportunity to teach Alexander just who called the tune in Europe. And, once bent on war, Napoleon convinced himself that Alexander was preparing to attack him.

He was firmly contradicted by General Armand de Caulaincourt, who had served as French Ambassador to the Tsar. By 1812, Caulaincourt was one of the few remaining Frenchmen who dared to differ from Napoleon. The Emperor evidently valued him for it, and as a result Caulaincourt was involved in many phases of the campaign. Finally, when Napoleon left his shattered army and sped back to Paris, he selected Caulaincourt to accompany him. Caulaincourt's *Memoirs* therefore provide a fascinating record of Napoleon's thinking, both before and after the disaster.

Caulaincourt claimed to have given the Emperor fair warning of Alexander's intentions. In 1811, when Napoleon asserted that the Tsar was afraid of him, Caulaincourt replied:

> No, Sire, because while recognizing your military talent, he has often pointed out to me that his country was large; that though your genius would give you many advantages over his generals, even if no occasion arose to fight you in advantageous circumstances, there was plenty of margin for ceding you territory, and that to separate you from France and from your resources would be, in itself, a means of successfully fighting you. 'It will not be a one-day war,' the Tsar Alexander said. Your Majesty will be obliged to return to France, and then every advantage will be with the Russians. Then the winter, the cruel climate, and most important of all, the Tsar's determination and avowed intention to prolong the struggle, and not, like so many monarchs, to have the weakness to sign a peace treaty in his capital . . .
> Hanoteau (ed.), *Memoirs of General Caulaincourt.*

According to Caulaincourt, Alexander even pointed out that

> Your Frenchman is brave; but long privations and a bad climate wear him down and discourage him. Our climate, our winter, will fight on our side. With you, marvels only take place when the Emperor is in personal attendance; and he cannot be everywhere, he cannot be absent from Paris year after year.
> Hanoteau (ed.), *Memoirs of General Caulaincourt.*

Caulaincourt's testimony is particularly impressive because he was not an enemy of Napoleon but a loyal follower; he even served as Napoleon's foreign minister when the ex-Emperor attempted a come-back in 1815.

Apart from Caulaincourt's *Memoirs*, there is an extended account of this interview in chapter 1 of Nigel Nicolson's *Napoleon 1812.*

A gleeful British cartoon celebrates Napoleon's disastrous Russian campaign of 1812: the 'Corsican bloodhound' runs from the Russian bears with a 'Moskow tin-kettle' tied to his tail.

The Tsar's prophecies proved remarkably accurate. The invasion of Russia turned into the kind of campaign that Napoleon and his troops were least equipped to fight. As we have seen, Napoleonic warfare involved the employment of a fast-moving army that lived off the country, struck deep into hostile territory, and within a very short time brought the enemy to battle; victory in battle was accompanied or followed by the occupation of the enemy capital and a negotiated peace. In campaigns of this sort, Napoleon's swift, energetic manoeuvres and the fighting spirit of the army were decisive.

But Russian distances were vast and, unlike western Europe, Russia was not fertile enough to support a large invading army; in the event, the Tsar's troops made the land even more unwelcoming by destroying such crops as the invaders might have consumed. Napoleon recognized some of the special problems involved, and organized huge supply depots close to the Russian frontier; but in practice the French supply system proved hopelessly inadequate. The slapdash methods of the past now took their toll, and through lack of food, fodder and medical supplies, men and horses died by the tens of thousands from hunger and sickness. Caulaincourt, though full of praise for Napoleon's gifts ('Never did any man combine such a memory with more creative genius'), saw that

. . . his creative genius had no knowledge of conserving its forces. Always improvising, in a few days he would consume, exhaust and disorganize by the rapidity of his marches, the whole of what his genius had created. If a thirty-days' campaign did not produce the results of a year's fighting, the greater part of his calculations were upset by the losses he suffered, for everything was done so rapidly and unexpectedly, the chiefs under him had so little experience, showed so little care and were, in addition, so spoiled by former successes, that everything was disorganized, wasted and thrown away . . . The prompt results of the Italian and Austrian campaigns and the resources those countries offered to the invader spoiled everyone, down to the less important commanders, for more rigorous warfare. The habit of victory cost us dear when we got to Russia and even dearer when we were in retreat; the glorious habit of marching ever forward made us veritable schoolboys when it came to retreating.
Hanoteau (ed.), *Memoirs of General Caulaincourt*.

Napoleon promoted the belief – still widely held – that his army had been defeated by the exceptional severity of the Russian winter. But while it is true that the wintry retreat from Moscow (combined with harassment from Cossacks and guerrillas) finally broke the Grand Army into fragments, Napoleon actually lost more men during the earlier part of the campaign – not through enemy action, but because the supply system broke down and the hard marching and summer heat wore out both men and horses.

Given the size of Napoleon's army, such losses were endurable – provided that the Russians could be brought to battle and defeated. But the chance, if it ever existed, was lost at Borodino in September, when Napoleon won a bloody but far from decisive victory. For the most part the Russians retreated – not, as legend has it, as part of a deeply laid plan to lure Napoleon to his destruction, for the Russian generals were far from agreed on the proper strategy to pursue. But the actual effect of their inactivity *was* to lure Napoleon on. He drove his exhausted army on to Moscow, hoping that the Tsar would feel obliged to negotiate rather than leave his capital in enemy hands. But, as Caulaincourt had predicted, Alexander refused. The Grand Army was left stranded, deep in hostile territory – a danger that had been present in earlier campaigns, and was now actualized in the worst possible circumstances. As a final misfortune,

Moscow was largely destroyed by fire on the orders of its governor, Rostopchin, depriving the invaders of the shelter on which they had counted. With winter coming on, Napoleon decided that there was no alternative but to march away – a march that rapidly turned into a retreat, and ultimately into a rout.

1813-14: what went wrong?

National Guard: voluntary militia; roughly comparable to Britain's present-day Territorial Army.

At the beginning of 1813, Napoleon's situation seemed serious but not necessarily hopeless. By calling up the National Guard and extending conscription, he raised a new army with which to face the Russians (whose forces were severely depleted by the 1812 campaign) and the Prussians, who had denounced their enforced alliance with France. Although victorious at Lützen and Bautzen in May 1813, Napoleon accepted an armistice that lasted from June to August. He later regarded this as a mistake, since the Allies were able to build up their forces faster than he could do. British diplomacy consolidated the anti-French states into a new coalition which was joined by Austria – an event that demonstrated the worthlessness of the dynastic link created by Napoleon's marriage to Marie-Louise. Despite a fine victory at Dresden (August), the French forces were steadily eroded. At the decisive battle of Leipzig (16-18 October), Napoleon's Bavarian and Saxon allies deserted him and the defeat of the French army spelled the end of his European empire. The invasion of France in 1814 found the defenders heavily outnumbered and fighting in a hopeless cause, although it was only under pressure from his marshals that Napoleon finally agreed to abdicate. Typically, he made even this the occasion for self-glorifying propaganda:

The allied powers having proclaimed that the Emperor Napoleon was the sole obstacle to re-establishing peace in Europe, the Emperor Napoleon, faithful to his word, declares that he renounces for himself and his heirs, the thrones of France and Italy, and that there is no personal sacrifice, even life itself, which he is not ready to make for the good of France.
Quoted in Correlli Barnett, *Bonaparte*.

Some of the reasons for the collapse of the Empire have already been suggested. Of these, the resentment felt by so many of Napoleon's subjects and allies was particularly important, causing the Prussians and Austrians to turn against him and the Dutch to revolt as soon as they dared. But, in the last analysis, it was defeat on the battlefield that ruined Napoleon; and this was brought about by a number of unfavourable military and political developments.

See p. 50.

Perhaps the most important was that both the army and its leader had deteriorated. As Caulaincourt suggested, overconfidence played its part in 1812, making it harder for the Grand Army to adapt to new circumstances. But this army had also lost much of the national character which had made it so dynamic from the French Revolutionary period onwards. A high percentage of Napoleon's best French troops were pinned down in Spain or employed to garrison the towns of Germany or other subject states; and, of course, Napoleon's constant campaigning also involved losses that reduced the number of experienced fighting men. By 1809, auxiliaries from the vassal and allied states were playing a substantial role in the Emperor's wars, and in 1812 they made up no less than two-thirds of the force that invaded Russia. Only when his foreign dominions had disappeared did Napoleon again command truly French armies; and then they were armies of raw conscripts who fought well but became worn down by the forced marches and other feats of endurance called for by the Napoleonic style of warfare.

The effects were equally apparent on Napoleon and his marshals, who had borne the strains for almost 20 years. Napoleon himself asserted that a general could only expect a few good years – and then forgot his own words and continued to ride pell-mell all over Europe, conducting one campaign after another while simultaneously running a great empire. With the years, he lost something of his energy and resilience, and his health – once near-perfect – became less reliable; two of his complaints, a bladder infection and piles, were particularly severe on a man who spent so much of his life on horseback or jolting in a carriage across a continent. He was unwell during the battle of Borodino, and perhaps on some other important occasions. The significance of all this is hard to establish, partly for lack of precise medical evidence and partly because the subject arouses intense partisanship: admirers of Napoleon tend to excuse his defeats on the grounds of health and age, and for the same reason anti-Bonapartists minimize these factors. What cannot be contested is that a military system

The sentimental side of the Napoleonic legend. On the night of 25 January 1814 the Emperor takes leave of his wife and son, whom he was never to see again.

This ingenious 'hieroglyphic portrait' offers a distinctly ▶
unsentimental contemporary view of the newly fallen Emperor in 1814.

GOVERNOR OF THE ISLAND OF ELBA.

J. Kay 1814

Description of the hieroglyphic Portrait of Buonaparte.

The French Eagle crouching forms the *chapeau en militaire*.
The Red Sea represents his *throat* illustrative of his drowning armies.
The *visage* is formed of carcases of the unhappy victims to his cruel ambition
The *hand* is judiciously placed as the epaulet drawing the Rhenish Confederacy under the flimsy symbol of the cob-web.
The *spider* is a symbolic emblem of the vigilance of the Allies.

so dependent on the well-being of one man must be unsound; and in that sense Napoleon's jealous concentration of power into his own hands can be said to have contributed to his downfall.

By contrast, Napoleon's enemies learned from their mistakes and greatly improved their military performance. The Prussians' reforms placed their army on a more popular footing. In Spain, Wellington demonstrated that well-chosen defensive positions and concentrated fire provided an antidote to the purely offensive tactics of the French. The Russian generals learned from Wellington and also exploited the natural advantages of the terrain. Napoleon's enemies slowly learned from him the importance of speed and energy in war, identified many of his characteristic strokes, and began to expect the unexpected.

In 1813 they also followed Wellington's advice – that, as far as possible, they should avoid taking the field against Napoleon himself, while striking at any forces commanded by his marshals. Then and later, Wellington declared that Napoleon's presence on the battlefield was worth 40,000 men to France. As this suggests, Napoleon's decline was only relative: he won some outstanding victories in 1813, and many historians believe that the campaign of 1814, fought against overwhelmingly superior enemy forces, was among his most brilliant achievements.

However, Napoleon's general conduct of the war in 1813-14 was notable for two omissions: he failed to concentrate his forces by pulling out of Spain and withdrawing the garrisons in Germany; and he repeatedly refused peace terms that would have left him the ruler of a still powerful French kingdom. The failure to concentrate his forces may have stemmed initially from overconfidence, but a more important factor was probably Napoleon's conviction that he could not afford to yield territory. The effect on French and European opinion of abandoning Spain, for example, would have been hard for Napoleon to contemplate – though, of course, we can now be wise after the event and say that the outcome could hardly have been worse than what actually happened.

The same considerations apply to peace negotiations – even if we assume that the allied offers were completely sincere. Napoleon expressed his own view in an interview with the Austrian Chancellor, Metternich:

In reality, the Allies' peace terms were never intended to be definitive: they were a basis on which fresh demands could be made. Perhaps they were no more than propaganda exercises. Napoleon had no monopoly of devious diplomacy!

Metternich, who wished to portray himself as the saviour of Europe, is not entirely reliable; but this statement of Napoleon's has the ring of truth.

I would die rather than cede one inch of territory. Your sovereigns born on the throne can be beaten twenty times and still return to their capitals. I cannot do that because I am an upstart soldier. My domination will not survive the day I cease to be strong, and consequently to be feared.
From Metternich's *Memoirs*; quoted in many books.

See p. 42.

There is plenty of evidence that Napoleon was right: his life and his reputation as a superman formed the entire basis of his regime. In 1812 the mere rumour of his death was enough to paralyse the imperial regime during the Malet conspiracy. On that occasion, no one seriously believed that Napoleon's baby son would inherit the throne if he was really dead; and when he abdicated in 1814 Napoleon's hopes that Marie-Louise might be appointed regent were soon dashed. The regime had no roots: its continuation depended on Napoleon's life – and on his continued success, which was the sole justification for his dictatorship. A negotiated peace which deprived France of all her conquests might not have cost Napoleon his throne, but it would certainly have made it impossible for him to continue ruling in his habitual autocratic style. This was shown by the demands for peace and freedom made at the beginning of 1813 by Napoleon's usually tame legislature: the first hint of weakness (his failure in Russia) was enough to revive a spirit of independence and criticism in

France. In 1813 Napoleon suppressed it, determined to remain master; but he could hardly have remained so unyielding after losing his empire. And he had neither the taste nor the temperament for constitutional monarchy – or so it seemed in 1813-14.

But see p. 56.

This is only to say that Napoleon's actions were not gross errors, but were dictated by the logic of his position – as he saw it. Whether they were in the best interests of France is another matter. And of course it is perfectly possible to argue that, whether logical or otherwise, his outlook showed the inability to come to terms with realities that characterize a man spoiled by success.

The flight of the eagle

Napoleon was an expert self-propagandist with a genius for 'theatre'. But with one side of his mind he believed most of his own propaganda, seeing himself as the incarnation of France, becoming drunk on the 'glory' and 'honour' of war, and viewing his own career as high romance, decreed by destiny. This 'romantic' Napoleon was never more in evidence than in the story of his return from Elba to re-claim his kingdom. The risks he took are a reminder that the picture of Napoleon as exclusively a 'calculator' will not do – though the unromantic may well ask whether the episode amounts to more than the final throw of a compulsive gambler.

After his abdication in 1814, Napoleon several times referred to himself as 'a dead man' – meaning politically dead, no doubt, though soon afterwards he did make an attempt to poison himself. He seems to have taken his failure to die as yet another decree of fate, and went with no more ado to Elba, the island granted to him by the peace settlement. On his arrival (4 May 1814) he undertook the administration of his tiny kingdom with his customary vigour.

Over the next ten months Napoleon's grievances multiplied; in particular, the new French king, the Bourbon Louis XVIII, had not paid the subsidy needed to maintain Napoleon on Elba, and Marie-Louise and Napoleon's son had not been allowed to join him. On the other hand, the European situation seemed favourable to a new adventure: the victorious Allies were quarrelling, and the Bourbons had made themselves unpopular in France by attempting to revive aspects of the Ancien Régime. On 26 January 1815 Napoleon left Elba in a single ship, accompanied by a handful of men.

Given Napoleon's miniscule resources and the great distances involved (about 600 miles from Elba to Paris), it was an extraordinary gamble. It might easily have been a fiasco at the very beginning, but Napoleon's ship, the *Inconstant*, successfully eluded British patrols and landed at Golfe Juan on 1 March. Napoleon avoided the royalist areas of Provence (where he had narrowly avoided a lynching the year before) and led his men through the mountains. Everything went with the miraculous smoothness of fiction or fable. Soldiers sent against Napoleon by King Louis changed sides and joined his party. Grenoble and Lyon opened their gates to him. Even Marshal Ney, who had taken service with the Bourbons and had sworn to bring back 'the usurper' in an iron cage, was carried away and rejoined his old master. Louis XVIII fled, and Napoleon was carried in triumph into the Tuileries palace in Paris, Emperor of France once more.

This episode is worth dwelling on because it tells us something of the emotional temperature of the period, which is easily lost sight of in cool analysis. It is important to understand the rhetoric as well as the 'realities' of an age – the thrill and force of the proclamation to the army, issued by Napoleon at Golfe Juan:

Napoleon's return from Elba – one episode in his career whose high-flown romantic quality is scarcely exaggerated by the artist who illustrated it.

Napoleon is now presenting himself as the saviour of France rather than the conqueror of Europe – a nimble adaptation to the altered circumstances.

Soldiers! In exile I heard your voice . . . Your general, made king by the voice of the people and raised to the throne upon your shields, has returned: come and join him. Renounce the colours which the nation has proscribed and which for twenty-five years have served to rally the enemies of France. Unfurl instead that tricolour which you carried in the day of our greatness! . . . Take up once more the eagles which you carried at Ulm, at Austerlitz, at Jena, Eylau, Friedland, Moscow . . .

We must forget that we were the masters of the continent; but we must not let anyone meddle in our affairs . . .

Soldiers, rally round the standard of your leader . . . Victory will advance at the double. The eagle, bearing the national colours, will fly from steeple to steeple, right to the towers of Notre Dame. And then you will be able to show your scars with honour, then once again you will be able to boast of what you have done. You will be the liberators of your country . . .

Quoted in Hutt, *Napoleon.*

Another example illustrates the way in which the romantic and the calculator in Napoleon complemented each other. On leaving Elba he realized that his only chance of re-establishing himself lay in getting to Paris without firing a shot: as soon as blood was shed, Frenchmen would be at each other's throats and, even if he managed to seize the throne, a disunited France could not possibly fend off her powerful enemies. This was the 'calculation'. But Napoleon's consequent behaviour could hardly have been predicted. Outside Grenoble, his party was faced by a battalion of troops sent by the King to stop it. Napoleon dismounted, walked towards the battalion, flung open his famous grey coat and shouted 'Soldiers! Here is your Emperor: kill him if you wish!' Ignoring orders to fire, the soldiers broke ranks and surrounded him, shouting 'Vive l'Empereur!'

So much for the high romance of the 18-day march to Paris, which became one of the great set-pieces of the Napoleonic legend. Whether Napoleon's return – any more than his earlier policies – served the best interests of France is more debatable, especially since his regime had only the remotest chance of surviving.

The final campaign

To Napoleon's disappointment, the European powers formed a united front against him. His peace offers were spurned and he was declared an outlaw – a position from which it would be difficult for any of the Allies to retreat. From a military point of view the situation was therefore just as bad as it had been in 1814.

In France, public opinion had changed in the course of a year. Many people preferred Napoleon to the Bourbons, but had no wish to live under a dictatorship again. Needing all the support he could get, Napoleon consented to an 'Additional Act to the Constitution of the Empire' which transformed him into a constitutional monarch. And so, in spite of his statement to Metternich, he had brought himself to accept a reduction in the size of his dominions and the nature of his power – though it must be said that he was ill at ease in his new role.

See p. 53.

Despite the gravity of his situation, Napoleon never seriously considered another option – to become a 'Jacobin Emperor', mobilizing the upsurge of popular feeling in Paris and other cities to conduct a 'people's war' against the invaders. Before Waterloo – perhaps even after it – this would probably have improved his chances, though the political consequences would have been incalculable. But Napoleon's lifelong horror of 'the mob' inhibited him, and although he now based his claim to the throne on popular consent, he chose to fight and lose his last campaign in strictly conventional military style.

In June 1815, Napoleon took the offensive in Belgium, hoping to destroy Wellington's Anglo-Dutch army and Blücher's Prussians, one after the other, before the Austrians and Russians arrived on the scene. The Prussians were severely defeated at Ligny (16 June), but not crushed; and they kept more closely in touch with their allies than Napoleon at first realized. He then pursued Wellington, who stood and fought at Waterloo (18 June). During several hours of fierce fighting, repeated and costly French attacks failed to break the Anglo-Dutch defences, and at the end of the afternoon the arrival of the Prussians turned defeat into a French disaster.

No attempt has been made in this book to analyse individual battles. Almost every encounter involving Napoleon has been exhaustively described and debated by military historians without any agreement being reached; and this is supremely true of Waterloo, which is re-fought with scarcely diminished partisanship by each succeeding generation. The fact is that, even more than most other events, battles are full of supposed blunders and hypothetical missed opportunities and alternatives that can never be satisfactorily weighed and counted.

On the other hand, it *is* possible to describe patterns of military activity, based on repeated strategic situations and consistent results; and this has been our approach to the triumph and decline of Napoleon's style of making war. In these terms, Waterloo is interesting as a crucial encounter between the French offensive and British defensive styles. The British style came off best – though Wellington admitted that 'it was a damned near run thing'. In other circumstances, with more time to manoeuvre, the result might have been different – but that is only one of many possible

In this fascinating piece of myth-making, bilingual (French and Italian) captions claim that the French were winning the battle of Waterloo, but that 'treason paralysed their efforts'.

The price of defeat: Napoleon's brother-in-law, the flamboyant cavalry leader Murat, failed to recover his kingdom of Naples and was shot in October 1814. Marshal Ney and others who rallied to their former chief were also shot.

hypotheses! Another point of interest is that at Waterloo the Allies showed how much they had learned from Napoleon: Blücher kept in touch with Wellington, making it impossible for the French to destroy the Allied armies separately. The threat from Blücher caused Napoleon to send 10,000 sorely needed men away from the battlefield in an attempt to hold the Prussians; and the arrival of Blücher clinched the victory – a Napoleonic concentration of forces on the battlefield, roughly comparable to the climax at Marengo.

After Waterloo, Napoleon returned to Paris, where he thought of continuing the struggle. But his own imperial institutions – the Senate and the House of Representatives – revolted at the prospect; and although his brother Lucien urged him to stage another 18 Brumaire, Napoleon could not stomach 'starting the Revolution all over again'. He abdicated for the second time, made rather half-hearted attempts to escape to America from the port of Rochefort, and finally gave himself up to the captain of a British vessel, the *Bellerophon*, believing that this gesture might persuade the British to let him live in England. He wrote a famous letter to the Prince Regent, declaring that

. . . victimized by the factions which divide my country, and by the hostility of the greatest European powers, I have ended my political career; and I come, as Themistocles did, to seat myself by the hearth of the British people. I put myself under the protection of its laws – a protection which I claim from Your Royal Highness, as the strongest, the stubbornest, and the most generous of my foes . . .
Dated 13 July 1815; quoted in Thompson, *Napoleon's Letters.*

The British were unimpressed, and Napoleon was sent to St Helena. The conflict between his imperial pretensions and the small-mindedness of the governor, Sir Hudson Lowe, provided the only drama in the remaining six years of Napoleon's life. But on St Helena he fashioned the legend of Napoleon, the benevolent despot and liberator, that has been examined at various points in this book. He died on 5 May 1821, probably of cancer of the stomach.

The years of repression in Europe after 1815 made the liberal-minded think more kindly of Napoleon, whose regime had at least had some progressive features. And when the restored Bourbons were again expelled from France (1830), a new royal line became reconciled with the memory of the Emperor, whose ashes were finally brought from St Helena in 1840 and reinterred with pomp at Les Invalides in Paris.

Napoleon on the Bellerophon, *which took him to St Helena. This painting by a late-nineteenth-century British artist shows how the glamour of Napoleon laid hold of even his former enemies; although corpulent, the Emperor is an impressive, brooding figure.*

NAPOLEON BUONAPARTE,

from a Drawing taken by Capt.ⁿ Dodgin of the 66.ᵗʰ Regiment at St Helena during 1820.

Published by H.B. Venna Printseller 157 Fenchurch Street

An irreverent contemporary British view of Napoleon on St Helena, based on a drawing made by an officer stationed on the island.

Conclusions

Napoleon: For and Against (1949), by the Dutch historian Pieter Geyl, gives a fascinating account of the way in which French historians of different periods and political outlooks have viewed Napoleon.

'Panorama of the Funeral of Napoleon', *which followed the return of the Emperor's* *ashes from St Helena to France in 1840.* *The event gave the Napoleonic legend a* *fresh impetus. Napoleon's tomb at Les* *Invalides is still one of the sights of Paris.*

The personality and career of Napoleon defy summaries and conclusions. The material is vast – hardly less than the history of early nineteenth-century Europe. Every facet of the adventurer-emperor's personality, and his every decision with its remotest consequences, has been minutely examined by historians. Each has fashioned his (or her) own image of Napoleon.

This book has looked at him from many angles, with no conscious bias. (As an exercise, readers may like to ferret out an *unconscious* one.) If there is any general tendency among modern historians it is to emphasize the importance of imperialist rivalry between France and Britain during the Revolutionary and Napoleonic period. On this view, Napoleon was essentially an 'agent' of the French notables, though an agent whose ambitions eventually outstripped theirs and actually worked against their interests. Historians of this persuasion emphasize the ruthlessness of the struggle, and point out that Napoleon was not alone in performing immoral

Panorama of the Funeral of Napoleon

actions – that, for example, the British navy's treatment of neutrals (including the bombardment of Copenhagen) was no more justifiable than Napoleon's border violations, and that his handing over of Venice to Austria in 1797 (often cited as introducing a new, lawless spirit into international politics) was a small-scale affair by comparison with the dismemberment of Poland only a few years earlier by Russia, Prussia and Austria. This use of comparisons is central to historical thinking, since we can only assess a person, event or institution when we have found out what is customary or 'normal' at the time.

None of this is intended to whitewash Napoleon, whose colossal egoism and love of power can hardly be denied. Yet, though few Europeans now have much regard for military strong men or imperial autocrats, Napoleon continues to fascinate, and to compel a grudging admiration. One reason is that he was much more obviously a man of extraordinary ability than (say) Hitler or Mussolini. Another is that he was a wonderful talker and, in his military-tattoo fashion, an impressive writer – one who adapted himself so cleverly to the occasion that his every statement has to be treated with care. His words served to express the multi-faceted personality that is at the very heart of his fascination – part-romantic, part-calculator, part-realist. For all his rhetoric, Napoleon could be remarkably clear-sighted about himself. He provided one possible summary of his career when a flatterer asked what Europe would say when the Great Emperor died.

'Europe,' said Napoleon, 'will give a gasp of relief.'

From Ajaccio to Moscow, from Egypt to St Helena: Napoleon's extraordinary life story still grips the European imagination.

Napoleon's Contemporaries

Alexander I (1777-1825). Tsar of Russia from 1801 to 1825. Joined coalition against Napoleon 1805. After defeat at Friedland and conference at Tilsit 1807 became Napoleon's ally. Successful war against Turkey 1806-12. After Napoleon's disastrous invasion of Russia in 1812, Alexander's armies fought their way across Europe, and he entered Paris in 1814. Liberal in outlook early in his reign, Alexander was a prop of the reactionary Holy Alliance from 1815.

Barras, Paul (1755-1829). French Revolutionary politician. Helped to overthrow Robespierre (see below). Suppressed Paris insurrection of 1795 with help of Napoleon, whose patron he became. Member of Directory 1795-9. Lost all influence after 1799 Brumaire coup.

Beauharnais, Eugène de (1781-1824). Son of Napoleon's wife Josephine. Served with him in Egypt 1798-9. Viceroy of Italy 1806-14. Commanded army corps in Russia 1812. After Napoleon's defeat, lived in Bavaria.

Blücher, Gebhard von (1742-1819). Prussian general. Long military career before served in wars against France, 1793-4 and 1805-6. Despite his advanced age, fought through 1813 campaign and at Waterloo 1815.

Bonaparte, Jérôme (1784-1860). Younger brother of Napoleon. Served in French navy. Married an American woman, but compelled by Napoleon to divorce her and wed German princess. King of Westphalia 1807-13. After fall of Napoleon, lived in Florence until 1848.

Bonaparte, Joseph (1768-1844). Napoleon's older brother. King of Naples 1806-8, King of Spain 1808-13. After fall of Napoleon, lived in the USA 1815-32.

Bonaparte, Louis (1778-1846). Younger brother of Napoleon. Married Napoleon's step-daughter, Hortense de Beauharnais 1802. Became King of Holland 1806. Abdicated 1810. His son became the Emperor Napoleon III 1852-71.

Bonaparte, Lucien (1775-1840). Napoleon's younger brother. As president of Council of Five Hundred 1799 helped Napoleon to take power at Brumaire. Quarrelled with him, exiled, and captured by British on way to USA 1810. With Napoleon during 100 days 1815.

Castlereagh, Lord (1769-1822). British politician, held many offices. As foreign secretary 1812-22 organized coalition that defeated Napoleon. Widely regarded as leading figure in repressive governments 1815-22. Committed suicide.

Caulaincourt, General Armand de (1772-1827). Soldier and diplomat. Ambassador to Russia 1807-11. Foreign minister 1813-14 and 1815 (100 Days). With Napoleon on return journey from Russia: his *Memoirs*, not published until 1935, particularly valuable.

Davout, Louis Nicolas (1770-1823). One of Napoleon's ablest marshals, victor of Auerstädt 1806. Minister of war during 100 Days.

Fouché, Joseph (1763-1820). French politician. During the Revolution, a regicide (one who voted for the King's death) and terrorist. Minister of police 1799-1802, 1804-10, notorious for efficient use of spies and informers. Dismissed by Napoleon for over-great independence, but recalled in 1815. After Waterloo, led provisional government. Nonetheless exiled after return of Bourbons.

Francis I (1768-1835). Emperor of Austria 1804-35. Also, as Francis II, the last Holy Roman Emperor 1792-1806, abdicating when Napoleonic changes reduced authority to nil. His daughter Maria Luisa (Marie Louise, see below) became Napoleon's second wife.

Frederick William III (1770-1840). King of Prussia 1797-1840. Weak king, under strong influence of wife, Queen Louise. Made war on French Revolution 1792-4 and Napoleon 1806-7. Kingdom dismembered after defeat, and almost lost his throne. State and army reorganized by able ministers 1807-12. Took part in victorious campaign of 1813-14. Part of reactionary Holy Alliance from 1815.

Josephine, Empress (1763-1814). Born in Martinique. Married Alexandre de Beauharnais, French general guillotined during Revolution. 1796 married Napoleon who adopted her children, Eugène (see above) and Hortense de Beauharnais. Divorced by Napoleon 1809 because she had failed to give him a child.

Louis XVI (1754-93). King of France 1774-92 when French Revolution began. Guillotined.

Louis XVIII (1755-1824). Younger brother of Louis XVI (see above). During French Revolution went into exile 1791-1814. King of France after fall of Napoleon 1814-15, 1815-24.

Marie-Louise, Empress (1791-1847). Napoleon's second wife, daughter of the Austrian Emperor Francis I. Bore Napoleon a son 1811. After Napoleon's fall, not allowed to join him. Made Duchess of Parma and provided with a handsome 'adviser' who quickly consoled her.

Metternich, Prince (1773-1859). Austrian politician and diplomat. Ambassador to Napoleon 1806-9. Foreign minister 1809-48, at first with policy of conciliating Napoleon and forming marriage alliance with him. Joined anti-French coalition 1813. After the fall of Napoleon, Metternich was the chief inspirer of repressive policies throughout Europe.

Moreau, Jean Victor (1763-1813). French general in Revolutionary wars, victor of Hohenlinden 1800. Implicated in conspiracy against Napoleon and exiled 1803. Lived in United States until entered Russian service. Mortally wounded at battle of Dresden.

Nelson, Horatio (1758-1805). British admiral. Victor at Aboukir Bay 1798, trapping Napoleon's army in Egypt. Defeated Danes at Copenhagen 1800. Victory and death at Trafalgar, which ended possibility of French invasion of Britain.

Ney, Marshal (1769-1815). 'The bravest of the brave', distinguished himself during retreat from Moscow. Became peer of France on restoration of Louis XVIII but rallied to Napoleon in 1815. Tactical commander of French army at Waterloo. After second abdication, tried and executed.

Paoli, Pasquale di (1725-1819). Corsican leader in struggle for independence against Genoa and France. Exile in Britain 1769-89. Recalled at French Revolution, led Corsican revolt against France and called in British. Retired to Britain 1796.

Pitt, William (1759-1806). 'Pitt the Younger', British prime minister 1783-1801 and 1804-6.

Pius VII (1742-1823). Pope 1800-23. Signed Concordat 1801 with Napoleon, at whose coronation he presided 1804. After annexation of Papal States 1808, imprisoned at Savona and Fontainebleu 1809-14. After fall of Napoleon, suppressed Italian nationalist movement.

Robespierre, Maximilien (1758-94). French Revolutionary leader. Dominant figure, though not dictator 1793-4, largely responsible for the Terror. Overthrown and guillotined.

Sieyès, the Abbé (1748-1836). French priest and politician. Influential pamphleteer during early phase of French Revolution. One of the chief organizers of Brumaire coup 1799. Became count of Napoleonic Empire. In exile 1814-30.

Stendhal. Pen-name of Henrie Beyle (1783-1842), great French novelist. Worked in imperial administration, travelling widely; the shadow of Napoleon hangs over his most famous novels, *Scarlet and Black* 1831 and *The Charterhouse of Parma* 1839.

Talleyrand, Charles Maurice de (1754-1838). French politician and diplomat. Bishop of Autun, but left Church and threw in lot with French Revolution. Foreign minister 1797-1807. Opposed Napoleon's expansionist policy, encouraging Tsar Alexander to resist. In 1814 helped to secure throne for Bourbons. Foreign minister 1814 and prime minister 1815. Cynical and corrupt, but a remarkable 'survivor': after another change of regime, ambassador to Britain 1830-4.

Wellington, Duke of (1769-1852). British general. As Arthur Wellesley, served in India. Commander of victorious British forces in Peninsular War (Spain and Portugal, 1809-13). With Blücher (see above), defeated Napoleon at Waterloo 1815. Later British prime minister 1828-30 and foreign secretary 1834-5.

Book List

Introductory works
There are many good short books about the French Revolution and Napoleon. Any one of the following would make a good starting point:

Elizabeth and James Campling, *The French Revolution*, Batsford, 1984

David Chandler, *Napoleon*, Weidenfeld, 1973 (especially good on the military side)

Nathaniel Harris, *Spotlight on the Napoleonic Wars*, Wayland, 1987 (a highly compressed account)

Nathaniel Harris, *The Storming of the Bastille*, Dryad, 1986

Felix Markham, *Napoleon and the Awakening of Europe*, EUP, 1954; Penguin paperback, 1975

Books quoted or mentioned in the text
Correlli Barnett, *Bonaparte*, Allen and Unwin, 1978

Fauvelet de Bourrienne, *Memoirs of Napoleon Bonaparte*, 1829; English translation 1831

David Chandler, *Napoleon*, Weidenfeld, 1973

Christopher Frayling, *Napoleon Wrote Fiction*, Compton Press, 1972

Pieter Geyl, *Napoleon: For and Against*, Cape, 1949; Penguin paperback, 1965

J. Hanoteau (ed.) *Memoirs of General Caulaincourt*, translated by H. Miles, 1950

Maurice Hutt, *Napoleon* (documents and extracts), Prentice-Hall, 1972

R.F. Leslie, *The Age of Transformation*, Blandford, 1964

Piers Mackesy, *War Without Victory: the downfall of Pitt 1799-1802*, OUP, 1984

Louis Madelin, *The Consulate and the Empire*, Heinemann, 1934

Nigel Nicolson, *Napoleon 1812*, Weidenfeld, 1985; paperback, 1986

Stendhal, *The Chartehouse of Parma*; many translations and editions including Penguin Classics series

A.J.P. Taylor, *How Wars Begin*, Hamish Hamilton, 1979; Futura paperback, 1980

J.M. Thompson, *Napoleon Bonaparte: his rise and fall*, Blackwell, 1952

J.M. Thompson (ed.), *Napoleon's Letters* (a selection), Dent (Everyman's Library), 1954

Leo Tolstoy, *War and Peace*; many translations and editions, including Penguin Classics series

Jean Tulard, *Napoleon: the myth of the saviour*, Weidenfeld, 1984; Methuen paperback, 1985

D.G. Wright, *Napoleon and Europe*, Longman paperback, 1984

Index